"Despite inklings of mild minded father and his thoughtful, flexible son, *Searching for Steve* chronicles the deep love between the two and their trust in and enjoyment of each other. Through the telling of his story, Steve emerges as a kind, brilliant, loving, and idealistic young man who believed in the power of knowledge to improve our world, and who desperately wanted to do his part by sharing his passion and knowledge of history with others. Steve's teaching journals are fascinating both as a glimpse into the challenges of teaching and as a glimpse into Steve's own hope and determination and creativity. I'm glad his father undertook the difficult task of sharing him with us."

— Laura Moher, author of the upcoming novel *Curves for Days*

Searching for Steve

Joel Harris

Apprentice
House Press
Loyola University Maryland

First Edition

Library of Congress Control Number: 2022950393

Hardcover ISBN: 978-1-62720-471-2
Paperback ISBN: 978-1-62720-472-9
Ebook ISBN: 978-1-62720-473-6

Design by Grace Noonan

Apprentice
House Press
Loyola University Maryland

Loyola University Maryland
4501 N. Charles Street
Baltimore, MD 21210
410.617.5265
www.ApprenticeHouse.com
info@ApprenticeHouse.com

Stories and excerpts from *Searching for Steve*
previously published by Joel Harris:

Memoryhouse Magazine, 2016, "In Search of Our Son"
Westview, 2003, as "In Nicaragua"
Northwest Review, January 2002, as "Jesus in Singapore"
Perigee-Art, 2008, as "Letting Go"
Dash Literary Journal, 2021 as "Do You Know Me?"

*In memory of my son, Stephen Neil Cohen,
whose dedication to his students inspired them to write such
heartfelt letters of condolence that I had to tell his story.*

*"It is in our power both to
bury adversity in lasting forgetfulness
and to remember what is favorable with sweet pleasure."*

On Ends

~Epicurus

Contents

Introduction

I came across my son's old Mac computer while rummaging through his belongings left behind in our cellar before he left for Nicaragua. Curious, I plugged it in and discovered he had kept an apprentice journal as a teacher-in-training and a record of his disappointing experience in a Long Island school system. When I shut down the computer, I was shocked by Steve's voice from the sound-actuating software, a message he had recorded several years ago.

"I'll be back," it announced, his mellow tone clearly recognizable even through the cheap speaker. Little did I know that Steve's disembodied voice would begin the search for my son—and for myself.

Stephen Neil Cohen arrived in Managua, Nicaragua, on July 27, 1998. He had a two-year contract to teach American and European History; specifically, he had to prepare his students to take the Advanced Placement College Board Exam in each subject. The American School had hired him the preceding winter after one interview in Boston. It was a serendipitous meeting. They needed a teacher to create the curricula and teach this vast subject. Steve, having just been let go in a Shoreham, New York middle school, desperately needed a job.

Despite problems in his previous job, the administration knew they had snared an excellent prospect and for good measure tossed in a new course in civics. What followed was the culmination of his odyssey to become a teacher... and his sudden and tragic death.

My wife and I went to visit him in mid-September, the beginning of his second year, one month before he died. The semester began in August at the American School. Classes were going well, although the newly appointed principal of the school, a former priest, had stirred up the teachers with new regulations. Steve, in a typical first-over-the-hill charge, had clashed with the administration. Rather abruptly, he was informed his two-year contract would not be extended past next June.

"How could they do that?" he asked me on an expensive long-distance call. He knew he had accomplished a lot that first year and it broke his heart. "I've done a terrific job. My students love me. Their parents love me. Should I go to their parents? They run this school."

"Be patient, Steve," I advised, ever the cautious parent. "There's plenty of time between September and June. Decisions can be reversed. Be professional. Hold your head up high."

"He doesn't know the first thing about education. He won't even let us use a lectern."

"As they say in the military, 'Keep your pecker up and your powder dry.'"

He laughed. "Well, Dad, it will be good to see you."

Ever the optimist, Steve was the kind of person who, at a funeral, expected the deceased to sit up and say 'hello.' I felt he'd be all right. Besides, there was a new teacher he had taken a fancy to, a young woman just graduated from college. He was a veteran, in his second year now, and could help her get acclimated.

"They're having trouble hanging on to teachers down here. It is not a hospitable country and the school doesn't make it any easier." He told me a story about one new teacher who went AWOL the next day after arriving in July. "No one knew what had happened to her; she just disappeared. Finally, the superintendent called her family at home to let them know she was missing, and who do you think answered the phone? The missing teacher. She made up her mind not to stay in Nicaragua the day she arrived. She didn't unpack, slept here one night and took the next flight out."

On the other side of immigration, the usual crush of eager friends and family waited to meet travelers from the States, mostly Nicaraguans returning home. We tourists were a distinct minority. I searched for Steve's face in the crowd, his auburn hair, perhaps a reddish two-day beard. He was over six feet tall with a broad frame and usually wore a shirt with bright colors—blue and yellow and orange. He stood out in any crowd. I didn't see him and was disappointed. We waited fifteen minutes outside the terminal.

"I got lost trying to find the airport," he joked as he ambled over from the parking lot, pigeon-toed in his worn-down-at-the-heel cowboy boots. "Haven't been a driver here for that long." How could you stay angry at him, bold in his shirt plumage, and handsome, like a red-bearded Viking, yet shy. We embraced, as we always did on greeting and farewell, with a special warmth and love. He was taller than me, a fully grown thirty-one-year-old man. But he had lost weight in Nicaragua, his finicky diet limited to what was safe to eat. He looked trimmer and quite fit. We commented on it.

"I walk my dog a lot." He had adopted his dog, Kinneson, as a junior in college, kept him hidden in the dorm for two years, lived with him a year in San Francisco after graduation, then back in Providence, where he completed two missing undergraduate credits and got his post-graduate teaching degree. Kinneson—part Husky, part Labrador Retriever—had adapted surprisingly well to the tropics. Steve loved his dog. Kinneson accepted Steve as leader of the pack, so Steve joked, because he had an opposing thumb and could open the door to let Kinneson out.

Steve drove us back into Managua with a sure hand at the wheel, hugging the middle of the road and traveling much too fast, for my comfort, in his old Toyota Tercel, maybe a 1987 model he had bought from his best friends at the end of the previous semester. They were a married couple, both teachers at school, who were expecting a child. They wanted to have their baby in the States, rather than a hospital in Nicaragua. We soon realized there was no logical road grid in Managua. It was a city without a center, a vast damaged slum of tin shacks, a few commercial buildings, open spaces with damaged overgrown foundations, a city destroyed by the earthquake of 1972 and never rebuilt. A few sturdy government buildings stood several stories high, and off in the distance we could see the pyramid shape of the Hotel Intercontinental, our destination. But how to reach it?

There weren't any streets leading toward it in a way resembling a route. Despite Steve's driving skill he hadn't yet learned his way around Managua, and he had a terrible sense of direction. I thought of Steve's story of the new teacher who left the next day and began to realize how she must have felt. But we were here to see Steve and the school and the community he had come to love in one short year. He had motivated students, both Nicaraguan and children of foreign nationals who were living in the country, and he had a challenging subject, history, to teach, working hard to create his own teaching format and style.

How, then, had Steve arrived in this place? Was it destiny? The working out of some grand design or was it just bad luck? In the 1990's senior high school history teachers had trouble finding a job. The system wanted math and science and special education. After one frustrating year trying to transplant himself to San Francisco, Steve returned to Rhode Island.

"What do you want to do with your life?" I asked him. He worked part time at our shipyard as a laborer. He didn't want to be in a family business, nor did I encourage him to be.

"I don't know, Dad."

"It should be something you want to do, something you get enthused about."

"Maybe teaching?" he asked.

"You can follow the family tradition there," I said. "Your mother is a guidance counselor. Your grandmother taught elementary school. And your stepmother taught art in the public schools."

"I would really love to teach history," he replied. I didn't realize he'd been working on his own history, a science fiction novel called *The History of Lathrim.* He had carried his notes and maps to whatever apartment he resided in, along with his dog, Kinneson, now four years old.

Steve enrolled at RIC, a long-established teaching school that produced most of Rhode Island's teachers, where he earned a graduate degree in history. Such passion and intensity are reflected in his journal, which describes a young teacher's odyssey in search of a career; his first practicum classes at Shea High School, his disastrous experience in Shoreham and finally a brief reverie on arriving in Nicaragua. They are a testament to teaching—the satisfaction of stimulating students to think for themselves.

In Nicaragua, he became the teacher he wanted to be, and the luminescent letters given to his sister, Laurel, by his own students after the memorial service in Nicaragua honor his brief tenure.

When Steve never came home I began to think more about who he would have become, which meant searching for who he had been—and who I had been. For 31 years I was Steve's nurturing father with a special curiosity to discover the man he might resemble. Could I fill that void by finding his birth father?

And who is my son's real father? Can someone who slept with a woman, whether a love affair of some duration or a one-off fertile moment never to be seen again, be considered a father? I knew a young man once, who told me the story of his birth—conceived by an unknown father at The Woodstock Music Festival. His mother bravely kept her child, nurtured him, raised him, and sent him off to school where he became an architect. She never married.

Just the reverse happened to Steve, who knew neither his birth father nor mother and relied on the nurturing of adoptive parents. When he was eight, we divorced and shared his custody—his mother keeping him during the school week while I took him in tow each weekend, structuring my life around him to provide the proverbial role model, until he went off to college and broke the invisible thread binding all three of us.

He claimed the best of both worlds, indulged by both parents during his time with each, suffering only from an absence of discipline. He loved us both, of that I am certain.

Yet I am also almost certain that his very nature, his innate gifts, overwhelmed our disparate love and indulgence. Because we were not a united front—mother and father living together and organizing his life in unison—Steve dominated each one of us through our divided but best wishes for his future. He was intelligent, scoring high on tests that could not be programmed by lesson learning.

I sheltered Steve. I bought him his first computer and sent him to university without any surviving debt. I bought and repaired his first second-hand car because Steve, a typical teenager, was accident-prone. I fed him sirloin steak on school vacation. I was uncle to his friends, bailed out his credit cards and parking fines, guided his increasingly stubborn way toward an academic life, my worries for him perfectly synchronized with my love. But I couldn't prevent him adopting a stray from animal rescue, a dog that grew too large and rambunctious for my home. For the love of dogs, he gave up his life. Ah, Kinneson, I could not shield my son from your love.

In *The History of Lathrim*, Steve created a separate world with its own Gods, peopled with races of humanity that were unique to his imagination. His words flow from teaching journal to essay, from heart-aching letter to his fantasy world. They are unique words which he used to make sense of the tenuous and shifting world imposed upon him—given up once for adoption, loved and cherished twice as much by parents whose own lives had changed and diverged.

Steve wrote that Saren, a child of the gods,

"Discovers new ways of doing things, that require more

than just an understanding of the natural order of the world; they require an understanding of how to actively alter it to achieve a goal, ways that go well beyond the simple faith in the world and the workings of it that Lithara, his mother, or indeed any of the Gods, could provide... Life was becoming more than just survival, and Saren provided a release for their passions, enabling individuals to express themselves through their own acts of creation."

Even as he grows older, Saren remains a child his entire life. Saren encounters different tribes in his adventures and tries to bring them new ways of thinking. He brings literacy so that they might write down the story of their people in order to learn from it. He shows others how to predict the weather so that their voyages might be safer. Some tribes he teaches how to fish, others how to plant crops. To the hunters he teaches the pictorial language in the caves in order for them to preserve their family histories.

There are many parallels between Saren/Steve in his story and in his own life, too replete with irony and prescience for me to even contemplate. Saren is often frustrated by the indifference of many tribes to the knowledge he is so desirous of imparting. He is often the butt of practical jokes. When he shows patience and good humor some tribes stay with him long enough to learn numbers, to keep score of games, and written language so that the "best" jokes would be remembered forever. Saren is destined, in Steve's story, to die young.

In coming to terms with the loss of my son, I discovered a hidden parallel in the life of a young woman I once loved, whose son and only child died in a tragic Paris subway accident. Her youthful idealism had connected us all through the years, reaching past me to influence my son to become a teacher. Did our lives follow a trajectory beyond our control? It is a central question for a father who wonders how he might, otherwise, have saved his own son's life.

Ultimately, *Searching for Steve* is a quest for the soul and spirit of a young man who has died too soon. Steve's odyssey brought him to a strange land, Nicaragua, where he did indeed find himself fulfilled, sharing his precious knowledge with students who were receptive to him and eager to learn. That he enjoyed some measure of success was enormously gratifying to him. He touched too few lives during his brief teaching career and that is a shame because he had a unique voice.

"I'll be back," spoke Steve's voice, fresh and innocent on the Apple computer, where he wrote his teaching files. And perhaps he will.

PART ONE
Dreams and Enchantment

The desire to learn and express that Saren brings to the
Therasan is so profound that many refuse to merely experience the God through the boughnet, they actively set out to
learn at his knee (or he on theirs, as the case usually was).
His teaching bough became a permanent place of learning,
the first such permanent community in Therasan history. He
creates writing so that each individual might express him or
herself as an individual. Saren brings literacy to the tribes so
that people might write down their stories. They learn numbers to keep score of games, and language so that the "best"
jokes might be remembered forever.

—*The History of Lathrim*

Chapter One

Lonely in Providence, Stephen lived for his dog Kinneson rather than a movie or dinner out with Sylvia, his stepmother, and me. I wished cleverness for him, the talent of Odysseus. I wanted him street smart, as well as book smart, to be practical in his life. A short time after his death, at age 31, I entered my own fantasy world in search of my son.

"This child has better genes than your own family," said my aunt, who was head of The Family Adoption Agency in Boston. From her, I had discovered the first clues to my son's origin.

"The father is tall, the mother average size. One has a complexion like Stevie.

"Both sets of his parents were college educated." One set had been to graduate school.

"More education than you had," noted my aunt dryly. "You may find that Stevie has musical proficiency. His paternal grandfather taught in the music department of a university in Providence."

"If Stevie ever wants to know about his birth parents, I'll help him find them. If I die (she was then in her late 60s), I'll leave their names with your cousin. She can help, but *only* if

Stevie wants."

I had asked Steve several times if he wanted to find them. "I'm not interested," he always replied.

It was as if my aunt had put an enchantment over my head, some enormous curiosity to discover who Steve might have become and whom he could have resembled. The adoption process allows some assistance in that for the child, but not for the nurturing parent. For me the file was sealed tight. After Steve died, I tried many times to find out who his birth parents were but was denied even a reflective glimmer other than the few tantalizing bits from my beloved aunt, who had passed on several years before Steve.

I could never say to anyone: I see Stephen in you. I see a unique talent that only you and he share. They are from your nature, your genes—not mine. It must be from you that he got his natural sweetness, his intelligence. But how could I tell them how much joy the gift of Steve's life has given me and at the same time tell them that their son has died in a tragic accident?

There usually is a first cause for someone to pursue playing an instrument—a parent who imbues their child with the love of musical expression and perhaps provided lessons to see if it might take root. There are special inclinations to talent—from Mozart's father driven to embellish the prodigy of his child to the head of a college music department whose son grew up surrounded by classical music and perhaps rebelled by playing drums in a jazz band.

Steve's nurturing mother could not carry a tune and his nurturing father could not dance. Raised in a home devoid of both musical culture and proficiency, Steve became a massive collector of compact music discs. He filled his own life with the sounds he loved, not just specific to the classic rock era he adored but ranging through the decades of his own life. And how prescient to discover that his favorite band was Rush, whose poet/percussionist Neil Peart also shared Steve's middle name, Neil. With his long dexterous fingers, Steve rapped a percussive beat to any song he heard. In all the world of rock music, he had chosen to admire a man who most closely resembled the father he never knew.

It was then that fate threw a red herring at me. The Arts Week section of our local newspaper had a picture of a man who promoted contemporary music in Providence at his nightclub, Henry's Heartbreak Motel, an appropriate name for someone who might nurture a deep regret in life. He started his club in 1975, seven years after Stephen was born. The newspaper reporter described Henry as a Scrabble® fanatic and word memorizer. He favored R & B music in his club and over the years had booked star performers past their prime—Muddy Waters, James Brown, Jerry Lee Lewis, and Roy Orbison. In the age of rock, rap, and hip-hop, he persisted in showcasing performers he admired.

"Eccentric as all get-out," wrote the reporter, quoting a close friend. In the promoter's own words, "I was the nerd at junior high school who brought his records to parties while everyone else was talking to girls."

Curious in my search to find Steve's father and thereby discover the man he might have become, I saw many similarities to my son—his obsession with collecting records and paperback science fiction books by the hundreds, a natural gift of excelling at taking exams, his awkwardness with girls. They shared a love of music from the 1950s through the 70s. I saw a resemblance to Steve in the two article photos. Both had high foreheads, with receding hair, and a strong jaw line. They each had a similar face shape—more rectangular than round, an even, straight mouth, large nose, and narrowing intense eyes as if shielding sensitivity to some otherworldly glare. And most coincidental, he had attended Bryant College from 1965 until graduating in 1971. Stephen was born in 1968.

I schemed how I might approach Henry; see at close hand if he resembled Steve. My wife thought me obsessed. I confided my suspicions to a close friend, also a bachelor, and a contemporary of Henry Perkins. He knew him. He also knew my son.

"They don't really look alike," he said, dashing cold water on my passionate fantasy. "Besides, he's much shorter than Stephen."

Unavoidable grief has haunted so many families. Time had not cured my own but rather, like a good tailor, stitched my life together once again. I meet Steve often in my dreams. With this story I try to bring Stephen back to my life, although he has never truly left me, not for an hour of any single day. I am greedy to know him better. I may have been father to Steve, but he was my teacher as well.

On my faithful Friday pickups, halfway to Stephen's residence in Sudbury, I meet my former wife in the parking lot at the Route 128 station for exchange of the happy prisoner.

"Hi, Dad," Steve says with a big hug and a kiss as he jumps into my car.

All the way to Providence, we chatter about his week, have a mac-and-cheese supper at Anita's restaurant on the east side and then home to my apartment. When Steve was eleven years old, I bid for a friend's portrait skill at an ACLU fundraising auction. I played squash twice a week with her husband.

"Whom do you want me to paint?" she asked.

"My son," I said.

He posed Saturday mornings for her, and in the afternoon Steve and I went to the squash court, and I taught him how to play.

Stephen looks confident in his portrait, done in early Renaissance style—like those portraits of young men behind whom a window opens onto a view of a mystical landscape of distant hills, somber in tone in contrast to the bright colors of the one posing. My young Viking son, with his reddish hair, truly looked like his portrait. He wore a blue and white jacket open to reveal a brown sweater with blue accents, a dark blue baseball cap perched jauntily on his head. Arms spread in a casual pose, he sat by a window that looked out to the image of earth in a dark void, as seen from the moon, clouds and ocean repeating the blue and white of his clothes. His left hand extended casually from his jacket, long fingers elegantly shaped, and in his right hand he held a Duncan Yo-Yo—a child who resided comfortably in the cosmos.

Chapter Two

In the year of your birth, I saw your father in every young man who fit my aunt's description. "The father was tall," she said, "six foot five, a college graduate." She hesitated, knowing the next detail was important to me, "and an athlete, well-coordinated for his height... He had brown hair."

"*You* are his father," my wife insists, whenever I refer to those two who conceived you. "I can't imagine I'm not his mother." And true, I love you, son, as my flesh and blood. I am your father more than that other could ever be although you are his flesh and her blood. They are abstractions—one tall, the other short: college educated, athletic, and musically proficient. You and I are as one, yet I hunger for their self-image more, perhaps, than you ever will. I would discover you through them, but instead I find them through you and you have a new surprise for me every day.

In the early spring, I thought I saw your father. At least I imagined you might someday look like this young man. The resemblance, though you were not yet a year old, was extraordinary. Moreover, I was in Boston, a city of half a million people where in fact one person, probably a student like him, was your progenitor, a statistic duly recorded in some bureaucratic file, and wisely they chose not to end your life with the freedom people seek today.

Could that young man have been your father? It was in Harvard's Memorial Hall and I was taking the graduate exam for the second time. He was as handsome as you. He sat at a table in front of me, those long exam tables in that familiar hall where I had filled so many blue books as an undergraduate. He was at least your father's height, six-and-a-half feet. What shocked me was he looked exactly as you might look when you grow up, fair complexion, tall but not skinny or stooped, rugged, with long legs and fine broad shoulders, good enough to be a sturdy end or a basketball center, or with those long legs perhaps a better hurdler than I could ever have been. You can see I already have you in training to become an athlete, to surpass me. You were born with the skills and you shall have my desire as well.

He had beautiful auburn hair just like yours, a high wide forehead and a full mouth—a confident expression, serene and smiling, I imagine loved as a child, as you are, my son. One's mouth tells the story of a face, of a person's entire attitude. I love your smile. But his nose was different: aquiline, aristocratic where you have a wide nose, so beautiful on your face. It suits you. It suits my image of you, flat and hard-nosed. You'll take your lumps as I have without complaining.

And there I sat, in that exam hall, struggling with math I hadn't used for years, three-and-a-half hours of comprehensive testing to measure me against—your father? What had I achieved since college? So little it seemed that I had to return to test myself again, go back to graduate school, to the path I should have persisted in. Your mother hoped I would be turned down. And perhaps secretly I did too, because of the strain it would place on our family. Wasn't I already a businessman? But I felt insecure, dangling in my own life.

You were not yet a one-year-old but you had captivated me and I could see you filling out enough as a baby to compare you to that auburn-haired boy taking the exam with me. What percentile did he finish in? If only I could at least compare his score to mine, measure us. The head exam proctor intoned: "End Part One. Do not turn back to Part One again. Read directions to Part Two. When I give the word, begin Part Two." I recognized the proctor from college days. He hadn't changed visibly during the intervening years. I remember senior year, the comprehensive economic exam I took in that same room, the high arched hall, brown walls and stained glass. My first error: I chose a graduate school in California. (Still the path led to you, my son.) After a summer of questioning values and two months of class, I left that school. Business education was not for me. Then, I made a colossal second misjudgment and went to work for my father and uncle.

Now, I try to escape by taking that test again, imagining your father sitting there. You will never work for me, my son. I will train you and build your muscles and your will. I'll lend you my experience and enough strength to go your own way; because you will be your own man. But my luck was about to change, had changed already when you came, bringing me another chance. Anyway, he is not your father. I am.

I remember that day in Boston, at the office away from downtown, a secret place where the two who conceived you could not trace your passing to another parent, could not wait outside to see what sort of family this child would have, fathom our potential as I have searched in my turn for theirs. And here you were given us, a treasure on a soft pillow—beautifully formed—but alas to me, a scrawny primate with flared nostrils, screeching for comfort, as I had seen your older sister once, all bloody and awkward, held up at birth by the obstetrician. You were six days past your own birth and fresh from the hospital, your face clean, not bloody. And your mother-to-be, like all mothers of mortal children, thought you were beautiful. And then we wondered whom do you resemble, enjoying the happy surprise of your fair skin and red hair. How many relatives would claim your look as theirs? We took you out the front door into that warm August day, walked carefully across Boston traffic to our car and caressed you all the way home. And I wondered what terrible responsibility I had taken on, what strange need to finally be a man for you to identify with. Especially with this unsure life of mine, this one long crisis past thirty, so frustrated in what I wanted to accomplish.

When you arrived your sister was eight. She was dear to us, too, and I felt I could never love another child as much. I struggled at my work. I moved material from here to there— scrap iron to the docks for shipment overseas, thousands of truckloads over ten years, a struggle to buy and a curse sometimes to sell when steel mills would not buy. It was exciting, though. My uncle had struggled through the depression. He kept profits under lock and key, forty years older than me, whom he regarded as a threat to his scrap iron rule. My rebellion sputtered for ten years, getting nowhere, as poor as when I began. But what else was I fit to do? I had a sort of power. I bought mountains of scrap, commanded men. You shall not follow in my footsteps—the first commandment of a father to a son.

No wonder we could not conceive another child; no doctor could help, no experiments with hormones nor temperature

charts, fertility experts, artificial insemination. Nothing worked
even when the spirit was willing. We were each healthy. But it
was a difficult time to be happy. Then you came, my son, after
only seven months. The agency worked faster than normal
time itself, faster than we expected. Thanks to that girl with
dark brown hair so unlike your own.

> *New snow melting in the high March sun cov-*
> *ered the ground fifteen inches over. He turned*
> *off the main road onto a plowed path leading*
> *across a field towards the woods and hoped it*
> *was frozen solid enough to support the car. They*
> *had been driving over a country road with snow*
> *plowed against the side and no place to stop.*
> *After a long drive, they had finally come to a*
> *path offering some privacy away from passing*
> *traffic. She leaned against him and squeezed his*
> *arm. They reached the woods which were only a*
> *narrow tree break separating the first field from*
> *another and entered on a panorama of the second,*
> *stretching perhaps a quarter of a mile to more*
> *trees outlining a series of hills. The afternoon*
> *sun had begun its long slant. It sparkled through*
> *the drops of windshield water and warmed the*
> *inside of the car. He decided to stop. They hoped*
> *a farmer wouldn't suddenly come upon them. He*
> *was improving at blind unbuttoning always in*
> *a long embrace working with his left hand like*
> *a pickpocket down her jacket, then her blouse,*
> *and as he touched her stomach she pushed toward*
> *him; and he kissed her neck again smelling the*
> *soap she used, so faint it could not be perfume.*
> *He reached behind to undo the hook, until her*

brassiere loosened around her neck like a bib. And
because it was too cold to undress, that was how
it remained. He took off his jacket and she unbut-
toned his shirt smiling at the ritual they made of
undoing one another's clothing. They smoothed
their warm skin over, two adept masseurs with
the delicate touch of lovers, feeling excitement in
the most remote place—a kiss in the hollow of
the collar bone, in the crook of an arm, a touch
below the shoulder blade. And like animals sleepy
with caress, they entered an unreal world in the
middle of a winter's afternoon, in the front seat
of an auto, oblivious to the awkward wheel, the
foot pedals jutting from the floor.

My father was very sick last year, suddenly an old man
lying in his hospital bed with white stubble prominent on his
ruddy skin, too ill to shave. Did I forget to tell you, son? He
once had amber hair like yours, now almost white. But he is
fair like you, his eyes blue-grey. He couldn't believe you had
red hair. Or didn't want to? It was too much to hope for, seeing
himself another generation away, immortality his through you.
He was an athlete like me and I surpassed him. Oh, to be like
you, my son and have many parents, a birth and a rebirth at
the same time.

My father loved you and this time my son I was thrilled.
He loved you—my surrogate reflection—and I in turn loved,
became more complete.

I kiss you in your hospital bed, father. Your white stubble
tickles my nose. You lie there with bottles high on their hooks
emptying dextrose and penicillin into your veins to keep you
alive, deathly ill with tetanus. Who knew whether you would

survive at seventy-two, no longer looking ten years less than your true age, an old man unable to swallow with paralyzed jaw and chest struggling to breathe. We stood in awe, fearing your demise and as, slowly day by day, you improved, I kissed you each time on entering and once again as I left. And knew you enjoyed this as much as I.

And, so, my father survived this time, three weeks in danger, six more to learn how to swallow again and talk, until later that summer he is well enough to eat solid food again, lie in the sun and swim, the gentle exercise of the old, cradled in buoyant salt water doing his patient sidestroke parallel to the beach.

But the summer ended in pain once again. He had a growth in his intestine. Now he had the dreaded disease that almost took his brother.

We were waiting for him to sign—the people who bought our business, aware of their good deal, feared a legal delay if he died, his second illness at a crucial time between letters of agreement and binding contract—the fine definitions that spell obligation, the metal market rising. Would he survive and sign? Would I lose a business and a father?

Mother once commanded her awkward boys to "Kiss daddy good night." He, too, felt awkward by the kissing. But as he slipped away, I felt the need to kiss him more, as if we could nourish him this way, passing food from mouth to mouth. And I know that at last he felt closer to me during this borrowed year we had. No business or misdirected ambitions to come between us. We had our blessing—his joy from my son.

As the nightmare I am having progresses, I want to cry because in it I am losing one pillar of my life. You lay in the upper bunk of my bed at the summer house. The room is dark, covers up to your neck. I see blood running between wooden slats below you. I, who usually sleep on the top, am standing next to you. I taste the liquid seeping through the mattress, confirm it is blood. You are dying. A fork is in my hand. The blood flows from your ribs. Can I hold it back like the boy at the dike? It runs through the fork tines and I try to save it because your life is seeping away. I urge you to live, "Please dad please." You understand and in your kind way say something humorous. You smile through my tears. It is so like you to be brave at death's door. "He took a long time to take me, didn't He son," you say. "I had a good life."

> They left their car in a cul-de-sac just off the
> road and entered the woods. Holding hands,
> they passed a steel pipe jutting from the ground
> that entered a small pump house. Beyond the
> contrived grove of pine trees spaced as even as
> a cornfield was the reservoir. Happy with one
> another, they embraced, then continued arm in
> arm across the soft pine needle mat. At the edge
> of the grove where the meadow began its slope
> to the water, they stopped and embraced once
> more. He spread his raincoat on the ground and
> they sat down. She arranged her skirt over her
> knees and looked across the water at the shore,
> surrounded by grass and the meticulous trees. The
> serene other world intensified desire. They lay
> down on the coat covering the pine needle cush-
> ion reassured by the feel of the other's body because
> it alone mattered, all responsibilities forgotten:
> odor of resin, the ground soft as a feather mat-
> tress. They scattered clothes to the side, green skirt
> from a distance a patch of moss, white blouse, and

pants gray as weathered wood, shoes and under-
garments took on a pattern familiar to the forest.

I notice an ad in the *Daily Gleaner* newspaper of Kingston, Jamaica, because it reminds me of my father's humility, driving his black Studebaker ten years until, beyond repair, we baled it in the scrap yard press. At times he was so self-effacing it hurts me to remember. He would say: "If business gets bad, I can always drive a truck." And I knew we could depend on him. He never expected wealth which still overtook him. He never let someone else carry his bags, too modest to live as a wealthy man. The ad read:

MUNICIPAL NOTIFICATION NO. 1874

"Separate tenders are hereby invited for the supply of coffins to be used for the burial of pauper dead: and hearses for the conveyance of pauper dead to The May Pen Cemetery. Materials used in the making of coffins must be of good quality and be approvedby the Municipality. The hearses must be in good condition with the drivers sober and suitable attired."

It is the way he wanted to be buried, in a simple box, his presence marked by a stone, lovingly remembered. He took little for himself and left us what he could. But I, unlike him, fear a pauper's burial because it means rejection by all who might once have loved me. I must guard against my compulsion to lose my family's love; to prove I am really not worth loving. Destroy their love for me by wrongdoing until one day on the bowery of my nightmares, in the New York of my father's early unsuccessful life, I would stumble drunkenly off a curb in front of a bus, no one to answer for me, lying in the gutter, because I had driven them all away years ago. A Calvinist fear keeps me hard at work. I smile at my pauper burial notice, put the paper aside and feel lucky to have had a son as the second child when I was closer to being a man. I needed extra time to find an identity to give him.

I follow you, beautiful son. "C'mon dad," you wave me to follow as we walk the Jamaican beach. A family vacation: we would not leave you behind. In the villa we have rented, you watch your sister read and demand a book in your crib at night. Identify with us all! And don't reject me, as I fear you might, as a young man. Will it be easier for you, not being my flesh and blood? Will you have to reject me to be a man yourself? You have resurrected me and I should be grateful for that alone, become a man to other men who don't discredit me but urge that I grow with them. I crave responsibility now. I need no, "Thou shalt not," to guide my uncertain instincts, no yearning for mystic survival to motivate my good acts. If only all men had sons, what inner power would be theirs, what peace in the world!

Through me, son, you have my father's disarming smile, his copper hair, a sturdy frame. I have to return early to work while you and mother and sister remain in Jamaica another week. The night before leaving, I dream of arriving in Boston with a pocket full of extra money which I urgently have to deposit. I search downtown for any bank realizing it is foolish to expect my own to have an office here. Why can't I wait until home, it's so nearby? Preserve your capital before someone steals it, a voice seems to say. A woman directs me to a bank. I introduce myself to a young vice president and ask if he can deposit to my account at home. "I know who you are," he says. "I just saw one of your checks that is clearing our bank." He pulls it from a stack like a magician finding the right card in the middle of a deck. I am amazed he should remember my name. The check is made out to The Family Service Agency. "No problem," he adds. "I know you have an account at that bank. We can deposit the money for you." We talk about my trip and, as bankers do when they accept a large deposit, he feels a need to be friendly. I realize how unusually tall he is. Basketball was his college sport, he says. He confides in me—a story about a girl he had fallen in love with as a student. I hear vaguely familiar facts about talents and her family. Three years ago they had an affair. (Around us, in the shadows of my dream, bank business continues as we confer like two businessmen gravely considering options.) I wonder why he must tell me this story… She became pregnant. They couldn't marry because of religion, and gave the child up for adoption through The Family Service Agency. He holds my check, mentions the name, but with a banker's discretion seems not to notice the coincidence. I feel sick. Will he ask if the money was a donation? Will he ask if I had adopted a child? Suddenly the revelation: his height! I have found my son's father at last. The check, strangely unreturned, is dated over three years ago. Why had the agency refused to cash it? Was my claim in doubt? I wait for him to ask if I had adopted *his* child. I measure him for signs of the future, for my son's look. And I fear the connection he will make, his demand: "I want him back!"

I must not lose you my son. I must hang on to you at all cost. You are my identity now. This fellow has no rights. He is a spurned lover whom I have replaced. He has given you up.

Terrified, I awake and for a moment do not recognize this

29

louvered room in Jamaica, a warm winter evening, lights outside on the pool. Whose bed am I in? Was I her lover? Are you mine, my son, or theirs, or every man's son? Are you her son that died and are reborn for me? I am so afraid of losing you some day. I wonder if I can be a man to you as you grow older. Will I have the courage to let you push me away? I see the possibility now, as if you want to let me know—enough kissing, enough hugs daddy. Later I'll come back and put my head in your lap. I'll pat your leg. Just be there when I need you. (I run to you in the morning when you cry. You bite me, my three-year-old because, biting, you hold on to me and feel secure.) Love me when I need your love, you seem to say, guide me and let me grow. And don't be afraid to lose me, father, because that way you will have me forever.

How lucky I am to have survived until now. Some strength, perhaps a vision of what my life could be, has kept me sane. Each man dies with his father, is saved by his son. There must be a God who plays his tune on us if we suffer pain enough to hear.

My son, you will have your freedom.

Chapter Three

In the Saturday morning *Journal*, under real estate sales, I came across a foreclosure on Armington Street, the very house Stephen lived in ten years ago when he rented the third floor and was a substitute teacher in the Providence high schools. Deutsche Bank had foreclosed on the old three-story aluminum-sided property in a lower-middle-class neighborhood. Cheap rent, it was all Steve could afford back then, just beginning his teaching career. The owner let him keep his adopted husky dog, Kinneson, in the apartment and that had made Steve happy.

I wondered what Deutsche Bank was doing with a bad investment on Armington Street in Providence, Rhode Island? And how had my son come to reside in Nicaragua at age 31, where his own life had been foreclosed at such steep cost to those of us who loved him?

I think rationally but dream in fiction. One night, several years after Stephen died, I had one replete with all those created images that provide a sense of immediacy to the best of dreams.

I am napping on a Saturday afternoon. My brother telephones in my dream and wakes me up. He says there is a wonderful surprise in store for me. And as I sit up still drowsy, still dreaming, I see my son in the doorway of my bedroom. He walks over to me.

"I'm back," he says. "I'm sorry."

"Sorry for what?" I ask.

"For making you sad."

He embraces me and tries to console me, for I am suddenly both uncontrollably sad and wildly happy, sobbing viscerally, not understanding what has happened.

I must know. "Where have you been?"

"There."

"In Nicaragua?"

"Yes. I've been married, living with her family. You'd have been delighted to know her."

"Why didn't you tell us?"

"She died of cancer. It's been four years."

"I'm sorry," I reply.

"That's all right; I can visit you now."

I wake in tears, realizing that Stephen is visiting me from another place—the afterlife.

Stephen *has* disappeared from my life. I know that he is gone even as I love the richness of my dream life with him. I am grateful for my dreams.

Stephen had a physical beauty I could not claim—hair, gold-tinged brown and auburn is an inadequate description. It covered his forehead down to his large, brown eyes, a most angelic three-year-old face of marvelous proportion—full lips and a broad nose with flaring nostrils. He was a lion cub, playful and aggressive, safe to nuzzle. On the plane to Jamaica, he toddled up and down the aisle making friends with everyone, all the more puzzling when, as a teenager, he entered a shy zone of the sensitive redhead with fair skin who both blushed and sunburned easily.

When my wife and I were divorcing, I went to my aunt to ask forgiveness, and she gave me her best advice. "Stevie is still so young. Share in his custody. Share in his life and all the key decisions that need to be made. Look out for him and for his benefit. Don't let your wife take him far away. You must continue to be a role model."

If my dreams are fiction, then my Jamaican story is a search both for my son's father and for my own life, betrayed like Joseph by the sale of a birthright, yet naively believing that one's future lay in selling it. And were the lovers, embedded in the narrative, more than just surrogate parents?

Stephen was born one year before my uncle sold our business. I felt frustration at not being able to take it over and the steep responsibility of supporting a family and, possibly, returning to graduate school. Why adopt a child at just that point in a complicated life?

I confess my life had been more controlled by the hidden dynamic of my wife's needs. It was her insistence to have a second child, whether by natural means or by adoption. Memory skates on such thin ice. We conjecture from concealed evidence, my explanation no more credible than one my wife might give. What is the truth then? Does any story, twice told, automatically become fiction?

Long before I discovered my wife was gay, I had an affair, beginning when we were both most vulnerable—she pregnant in her eighth month and me sexually frustrated. Yet that was nothing new. My frustration had been a constant for the first two years we were married, my wife the most determined of virgins, coerced by family and her normal mothering desire to get married. Pretty and intelligent, as she was, an only child from a good family, she seemed the answer to a 22-year-old young man's dreams, and I the answer to hers, as I appeared to have prospects.

I believed my wife wanted to preserve our marriage, binding me to a contract with not just one, but with two children. I loved my daughter and had a nurturing instinct. When she was eight, it was time to seal my fate with another child. And even my future job prospects seemed to have improved. As my wife concealed her secret life from me, I felt driven by needs I did not understand. I found a willing and passionate accomplice.

In dreams, I imagined the lovers meeting surreptitiously— the birth parents of Stephen, this miraculous child given to undeserving parents. Our affair, hidden from both spouses, continued off and on during those early years of marriage until she became pregnant—by me. The trauma of an abortion sealed the end of our relationship, permanently.

Dreams, then, had special meaning, thinking I might atone by adopting another man's child. Still, why did my wife not consider the responsibility she so rashly assumed—raising a child in a relationship that carried the seeds of its ultimate destruction? We were two sexually misaligned souls whose hearts did not beat as one, to misquote John Donne.

PART TWO

Observation: How Teachers Teach

Saren gave each race the tools they would need to survive without the constant worry of extinction, so that individuals might express themselves through their own acts of creation, a creation as profound as the original creation that brought them to this world. Saren heals the leader of one of the most prominent families, the Checha, and while this immediately starts a fierce debate among the other families as to whether this sort of life-saving healing violates the codes of honor by which they live, it gains him immediate acceptance into the Checha family as a Son of the Wind, an honor never before conferred upon a non-Dalkani.

—*The History of Lathrim*

Chapter One

In 1992, three years after graduating college, Stephen wrote a letter to his ex-roommate and closest confidant:

Hi George,

You know, I haven't written *anyone* a letter in, god, it must be ten years. It feels strange. I was just taking Kinneson for a long walk in the park, feeling a little out of sorts, and decided that it would be a perfect time to write to you. You know, the one good thing about writing letters is that you can engage in these long, rambling monologues, and no one can interrupt you. SO prepare yourself.

I was just thinking about loneliness. I have no idea what it must be like for you living in Russia day by day, but I imagine it must get pretty lonely after a while. Well, let me tell you, it's kind of like that here too. You know, I think that that's one of the things we have in common, one of the things that binds us to one another—basically, we're both pretty

solitary people, and, despite any attempts
to combat it, that trait sometimes leads to
loneliness. It's kind of strange to think that
we have that in common, since we handle it
in such different ways. You tend to be very
outgoing and easy to get acquainted with, I
have a habit of hiding behind my idiosyn-
crasies, but both are ways of dealing with the
fact that we're both pretty closed individuals, not easy to get to know. I don't think
that it's bad, or particularly rare, but it is an
unspoken bond we share. I'm not sure why
all this comes up now, except that I happen
to be feeling a greater sense of loneliness and
longing right now than I usually do. Don't
get me wrong, I'm not going off the deep
end (or even the shallow end), in fact, I'm
basically content with my life, yet there's this
constant nagging in the back of my mind that
there's a difference between contentment and
happiness.

You know, for the past three or four months
I've had more of a life than at any other point
in my existence. I've been working about forty
hours a week, in addition to going to four
classes (3 graduate level), and I've managed
to juggle it all pretty successfully. My grades
are the highest I've had since fifth grade, I
actually enjoy the classes (for the most part),
and everyone at work seems to like me and
the job I'm doing, too. What's surprising is
that it is this very success in my life that has

brought on this particular wave of introspection (I thought it was only failure that made us contemplative, oh well, another theory out the window). Why? Because I've been forced to ask myself the question—is this all?

You know, I can picture my life five or ten years down the line. Teaching at some high school in some suburb (hopefully on the West Coast), living in an apartment with my dog(s), spending most of my free time reading, following the news, and writing, either about my world, or other forms of SF/fantasy (see below for more on that). And I think that all that will be quite enjoyable for me. I'm serious when I say I think I've found my calling in teaching, even though I've never formally done it in my life. The only two nagging problems I have with it are money and lack of advancement, and I think that the money problem will solve itself (either through family or some other source), and the frustration of having what is essentially a dead end (and I mean that in the best possible way) job, I can channel into my writing and world. So I'm quite optimistic about where I'm going (with that faithful, unbreakable optimism which only I am capable of generating), but I'm still left with this question of will I be HAPPY?

For a person who's so solitary I'm surprised at how much I crave human contact. Sometimes

it's just being in the presence of other human
beings (thank god for Kinneson, he gives
me an excuse to go out and interact with the
world without looking or feeling like a nut),
but other times it's for the closer contact with
friends. I must talk to James three or four
times a week, in conversations ranging from
ten minutes to five hours, and, although the
contact isn't as frequent, I talk to Elisabeth,
Natania, and Brett a hell of a lot as well. I
truly wish you were back in the States just for
the selfish reason that I could add you to my
calling circle (MCI LOVES me). It's amazing how little gets said for all the time I'm on
the phone, we go off on all sorts of tangents
and interesting explorations without really
talking about much (you'd be amazed at some
of the bizarre conversations I've had with
Brett). I can't imagine what it would be like
without having these people to talk to, at least
occasionally.

When I was incognito in San Francisco I
spent all the time I possibly could with the
news, just so my brain would have something
to cogitate about. I imagine it would be the
same in Providence. But that only points to
the real problem I have here—I don't know
anybody. It's amazing. I've lived here for two
years, and I still don't know anybody. I've
worked at maybe fifteen different jobs over
that span, I've played squash, and now I'm
going to school again, and still I don't have

any local friends. It's not that I've made the effort and failed, it's just that I've never felt that it was the right place, or the right time, or the right something or other, to make any. Actually, I don't really know why. The great thing about college, and the main reason I feel so good about my college experience (even though academically it was close to a nightmare) is that I made the best friends of my life, and I didn't have to work to do it. I just got thrown in with you people and, ala-cazam, instant friends. Not that it hasn't been work, since then, KEEPING my friends, but at least the initial effort was made for me.

Now, here I am out of the college environ-ment, and I don't know how to do it again because I never had to do it in the first place. You know, I had friends in high school, peo-ple I hung around with and argued with and had fun with, but I was never as close to any of them as I am to you people. In fact, here I am, only about an hour away from where I grew up, and I've only called them once, when I first moved back, and I don't really feel the urge to do it again, and from what I can tell, neither do they. I'm not doing any revision-ism of my high school days, what I had then were GOOD friends, without having any real CLOSE friends. Now I'm wondering if I will ever be able to get back into that "friend making" mode.

You know, it's strange that I have such a barrier there. On the one hand I get along very well with people I associate with. EVERY job I've ever had, EVERY one, the people who I worked for found me to be a pleasure (I'm not being immodest here, it's just the truth), even when I had to deal with agitated individuals, people were amazed at my ability to soothe ruffled feathers. When I am forced to go to a party of some kind (and I do have to be FORCED) I can small talk with the best of them. Even in class, I speak out more than any other ten people in the room, and I actually like giving oral reports (though that is a fairly recent development). Yet, despite all that, I am incredibly shy and find it damn near impossible to MEET people. That's one of the things I've always envied about you, your ability to react to any social situation and implant yourself firmly in it. I have no idea how you do that, I don't know if you do either, I think it's an acquired characteristic. But the fact remains that I basically lack some crucial social tool, the ability to speak to someone in such a way as to form a link that has the potential to grow stronger (there, that's a nice clinical way to put it). This applies equally to both men and women.

I guess that's what it comes down to more than anything else. Forgetting the men for just a minute, I just can't meet women. That picture I painted earlier about my life in five or ten years, I always pictured that I'd be married with kids, it seemed impossible not to be the case, but now I'm beginning to feel the first gentle hints of doubt. It's not that I don't want it; in fact, I want to get married and have kids more than any other single thing that I can think of. It's just that I have no idea how I'm going to get from here to there. I just want to *BANG* be married and get it over with. I know that's a hopelessly stupid and unrealistic attitude, but I just can't see what the alternative is. And, I have this quiet fear that the real difference between whether I'm going to be married in my life or just content lies with whether or not I can ever make this happen. I just don't know.

But, hey, enough downers. Like I said, it's something I think about, but not too often. Most of the time I'm either enjoying myself or bitching because I have too much to do. Right now I'm working on an interesting project. I've started yet another revision of my history system and this time I'm going all out. You know how I have my history set up in calendar form, right? Well, I decided that the best way for me to truly devise a history of my world is to construct a calendar of history for the real world, and see what parallels I could draw, what developments I had to explore, and some different impacts of different structures that I hadn't realized before. It started out as a purely technological

43

document. When did cities first develop? Written language? The wheel? When was the Bronze Age vs. the Iron Age? All those sorts of things. But lately it's kind of ballooned far beyond that and my simple calendar of pivotal events in history before 1 AD has now grown to sixteen pages, with no sign of stopping. But don't get me wrong, I love every minute of it. You'd be amazed how much history went on before, say 1000 BC and how many changes civilizations had to deal with. Which brings me to my new special project.

I was working on the calendar when I had a revelation. You know written language was created about five thousand years ago by the Sumerians, who had, by far, the most successful and largest civilization of that age. Written language made a tremendous impact on their lives. It allowed religious dogma to be preserved in its original form, it expanded the possibilities for trade and commerce immensely, and it allowed cities and governments to perform far more complicated functions than that which could be before. But written language was not widely disseminated. In fact, most of the rich and powerful people were, themselves, illiterate.

Language created a new class of citizens, the scribes, whose job was to use the new tool of language in whatever way they were told. Scribes were never thought of very highly in the society, in many cases they were slaves and treated as such, but their power, realized or not, was tremendous, as they controlled the language. Now, step back from that for a moment. Think about cyberpunk (don't worry; I will tie all this together). What is the basic idea behind cyberpunk? The world has advanced into a post-industrial age, an information age, and people are basically unhappy because it requires a major paradigm shift, and that's never fun. The world is full of users, people who understand at least part of the new reality and exploit it at the expense of those who don't have a clue, and these people are in conflict with those who have fully made the shift and are trying to get others to do so as well, a task made harder by these "users" who give meaning to people's fears about the future. This basic idea is then wrapped up in your standard plots and executed through a writing style that has become as completely stylized as film noir. NOW, and this is the fun part, combine the two. Write a story, or a book, in completely stylized Cyberpunk, about the scribes of ancient Sumeria. It's not as outrageous as you might think. After all, what, essentially, did the scribes do? Through the use of written language, they inserted themselves into the information flow, made themselves an intrinsic, indeed essential part of it, and best of all, they did it invisibly, without those in power ever really knowing that they were no longer in control. SCRIBES WERE THE FIRST HACKERS. Treat them as such.

Anyway, that's the basic idea. I think it has potential. Only now, in order to do it right, I have to find out everything I can about ancient Sumeria, especially the day to day life (walking down the dark, narrow, moon-drenched streets of Ur...), and, more distaste-ful, I have to read enough cyberpunk to get a grip on the style. But I think the whole thing has tremendous potential fun written all over it.

Other than that life's just fine. James is doing pretty well too, though I think he'll be glad when Angela gets back from her tour (which is soon). She must be going stir crazy out there—she even sent me a couple of post-cards. Give him a ring or send him a note sometime, I'm sure he'd love it. Oh, by the way, Mike and Sarah are getting married on May 30th in Massachusetts. I don't know if you got an invitation, if you didn't I'm sure it's because Mike didn't think there was a snow-ball's chance in hell you could make it. Well, its quarter of five in the morning, I'd better sign off. This has been fun; maybe I'll do it again before another ten years goes by.

Miss you,
Steve

Chapter Two

Stephen's first journal began by observing Ray McKnight's US History class at Shea High School, describing how McKnight related to his students in a friendly but still authoritarian way, generous with his praise but also demanding of class discipline. McKnight had a theatrical flamboyance that Stephen admired yet he always kept the spotlight focused on his students. It was early in September 1994. Miss Hill was Steve's advisor and also head of the History Department at this urban high school with predominantly inner city students. Classes were tracked from those studying World History and college bound, down to kids who were not likely to even finish high school. Miss Hill had given Steve his first class to teach—World History— taught by Miss McVeigh who was tackling the course, herself, for the first time, even though she had 20 years of teaching experience. She would stand aside and let Steve teach; then advise and grade him in the process.

McKnight, McVeigh, Hill, and my wife, Sylvia, had all become teachers in the city's school system at about the same time. That fall she had asked McKnight and the department head, Miss Hill, to take on Steve as a teacher-in-training. They had accepted, knowing he was an apt and dedicated prospect.

Sylvia knew all three teachers, having taught in the same school system for 15 years before retiring. She had, in fact, grown up next door to Ray McKnight, each an only child and a surrogate brother and sister to each other. He played football in college and besides teaching American History, also coached football and hockey. The unmarried Miss Hill, a cynic after teaching for 20 years, was also the most sophisticated of her contemporaries. She disciplined like the wicked witch and longed for college-bound students as intelligent as Steve. She appreciated him the most and ultimately saved his career. McVeigh's father owned the oldest Irish bar in the city. Fiercely Catholic, McVeigh had the least understanding of her academic subject and little respect for the natural abilities of her class.

Steve loved history—all the trends of human endeavor that brought the first hunters, farmers, and traders together into small communities. History's canopy spread over every subject, and he was bound to discover what dynamics drove society. It was a love he discovered after he graduated college, still shy two credits. He took his traditional walk through the graduation line, but didn't receive his official diploma until a year and a half later.

After one frustrating year trying to find a job in San Francisco, Stephen returned to Rhode Island and finished up his missing credits. The final paper he wrote had a Darwinian theme: *Thank God for Evolution*, a title he borrowed from a billboard, advertising the local zoo, depicting a flying dinosaur. The ugly creature stood both for the continuity and curiousness of life with an implied "Thank God" for evolution, which led to humankind, and didn't stop with this reptilian species. Part biological history, certainly irreverent, the billboard stimulated a reaction from the religious authorities who failed to see the humor, considering it a sacrilege to mention God and dinosaurs on the same billboard. Steve, in a kind of evolutionary dialogue with himself, wrote an articulate paper that clinched his degree.

Stephen had purpose. He was proud of finding something he wanted to excel at—teaching.

Chapter Three

IN THE BEGINNING: I'm observing Mr. McKnight's US History high school class for B-level students. My stepmother is an ex-teacher (art) and she has known Mr. McKnight for years, so he's very welcoming to me. I ask him about the class and he tells me that, despite the B-College grouping, this is a very diverse class in terms of actual achievement level. He also encourages me to speak up in class if I have something to say, although I don't intend to do much of that. He tells me to find a seat, and then tells the class that I'm going to be observing for a few weeks, then goes immediately into his spiel. The desks are arranged in five rows of six, making talking between students, at least when uninvited, rather difficult. Another problem with observing the social life of the classroom is Mr. McKnight's style—he's very LOUD. It's a good kind of loud, the kind of loud that says "WHAT I'M TELLING YOU IS IMPORTANT!" Nonetheless, this works for Mr. McKnight as he continually paces around the classroom, sitting on desks, and making himself very visible to everyone. The format revolves around the readings of the night before, with Mr. McKnight leading a discussion of what

51

was said and what it means. I'm surprised at the level of student involvement in the discussion. I would expect less from a group that is pegged at slightly below average, but the discussion is lively. The topic is the changes in foreign policy that occurred during the Roosevelt era (Teddy, not FDR), and the discussion ranged from the new role of trade to the increased American militarism. About two thirds of the class is involved in the discussion to some degree, though it is dominated by about three students.

WHO I PICK: I've decided to focus in on one student named Bernaldo. The reasons for this are many—first, he sits right in front of me and is therefore easy to observe. Second, he is not one of the students who participated in the discussion very actively, and later talks with Mr. McKnight reveal that he is at the lower end of this class in terms of achievement. Third, he is Black, actually from Puerto Rico, and, though his command of the English language seems very good, it is not his first language, and he seems a little uncomfortable with it. We'll see where this goes.

SECOND SESSION: I've noticed that Mr. McKnight spends the first five minutes or so out of the classroom, giving the students time to settle in and get comfortable, he says, so this affords me an opportunity to observe Bernaldo in a more social environment. He spends his time with three other students. I find out later their names are Charlie, Carlos and Patrick—all Black, but with different backgrounds. They sit in different parts of the room during class, so they don't have much chance to talk then, but now they are engaged in a rather lively discussion of some Sega Genesis games, and which of the new games are better—Mortal Combat or Street Fighter II. About this time Mr. McKnight comes in and the group disperses into their seats. The topic of the class discussion is a speaker who had been in the day before. He's a candidate for the Pawtucket school committee, and he spoke to two of the classes. The discussion this time starts out more slowly, because Mr. McKnight is asking the students about their own opinions of the candidate, but, once it gets going, it really livens up. One of the biggest areas of discussion occurs when the idea gets raised that he seems to be a very typical politician, and here even Bernaldo gets involved. When asked what was meant by a typical politician he replied that he kept talking about what he wanted to do, even if no one asked about it. Mr. McKnight agrees with this point, and Bernaldo gets one of his patented handshakes. This is an interesting interaction because, while most students act a little condescending towards Mr. McKnight when he shakes their hand, you can tell that it really has a positive effect on them—they straighten up, and pay more attention, and Bernaldo is no exception. The discussion turns to other topics, such as what he might want to do about it. Bernaldo, who spent a lot of time in the first class looking bored, seems much more animated in this discussion and, though he doesn't offer up any more direct responses, he does nod or acknowledge when he agrees with a point, and he raises his hand when Mr. McKnight asks who wouldn't vote for him. At this point the class ended and everyone was out of the room real quick.

THIRD SESSION: I looked in on the class again before the actual lesson started, and Bernaldo was talking to the same three guys, this time about a comic book called "The Pitt." By this point Bernaldo has become more familiar with my presence and we exchange greetings—I even get a new nickname—Steve Doggy Dog (a reference to a popular new Rap star named Snoop Doggy Dog). Class starts and I decide to focus on what Bernaldo writes down in his notes. Mr. McKnight is very explicit about what he wants in the notes, but I notice that a lot of students don't seem to write down what he says they should. Bernaldo is one of them. I notice a lot of drawings in his notebook that look like masks. As he's leaving the class at the end of the period I ask him about them, and he looks a little sheepish and tells me they're from the Mortal Combat game—part of the intro. I think they look pretty good, but now I'm getting ahead of myself. The class is on the rise of the temperance and suffrage movements as examples of progressive era reforms, and Bernaldo seems to spend most of his time thinking about something else—no notes and no participation. The only exception occurs when Mr. McKnight begins to compare the two branches of the suffrage movement to Martin Luther King and Malcolm X. He asks about the philosophy of the two men and gets a lot of loud responses from many quarters, including Bernaldo. After settling the class down, he manages to get some coherent answers and then compares them to the philosophies of the suffragettes. Bernaldo seems to pay attention to this part, and even takes a few notes on the comparison, but once the topic turns away from this he begins to lose interest again. Mr. McKnight goes on to talk about other progressive era reforms, but it isn't until the end of the class, when Mr. McKnight specifically lays out what the outline of the stuff was, that Bernaldo again takes academic notes.

FOURTH SESSION: I asked Mr. McKnight about Bernaldo's performance on tests so far and am a bit surprised to learn that he's pulling a solid B−/C+. Mr. McKnight thinks that he's less responsive in class because he's still uncomfortable with the language, but he does seem to understand what's going on better than I might have guessed. I also found out that Bernaldo has painted one of the flags on the wall—the Puerto Rican flag, naturally. Mr. McKnight's walls are filled with student artwork related to history for which they are given extra credit. One wall is entirely devoted to flags, and students from different countries or backgrounds have painted their own flag on the wall. Other artwork includes an illustrated speech by MLK Jr., as well as lyrics from Billy Joel's song about the Vietnam War. I spoke to Mr. McKnight about this during the beginning of the class, so I miss any early interaction that might have taken place, but I get a "Hey—Steve Doggy Dog, 'sup?" from Bernaldo when I walk in. The topic of discussion today is the Harding era, and, while the class is quite animated and lively, there is not much discussion, and everyone, including Bernaldo, is writing down notes. I think this has something to do with the fact that there is a unit test coming up and everyone is a little more aware of why they're there because of this. I decide to study the rest of the class during this time, to get a feel of what else might be going on while I'm here. Again I'm surprised how little horseplay goes on during this class, especially at this level, and how little talking there is that's not part of the discussion. I also notice that, during these four sessions, there has never been anything even faintly resembling any kind of disruptive behavior, and most of the kids seem to like Mr. McKnight. I've noticed before that he takes an interest in kids' activities out of school, especially sports, and he makes a point to greet each student at the door, with his familiar "Always a Pleasure!" I think this helps him to connect with the students, and makes them more comfortable in the classroom.

FIFTH SESSION: Well, today was the review for the test, and, because this is always an informal thing in Mr. McKnight's class, he suggests that I might want to take the opportunity to study more one-on-one with Bernaldo. I jump at the opportunity and ask Bernaldo if he'd be willing. He says sure, but then his friends start asking if they can go too, and I end up taking the whole group of four across the hall to the Resource Center. They seem to think it's some kind of privilege to get this kind of personal attention. We sit down and start to review the material, but I certainly don't have Mr. McKnight's control, and before long they're talking about one thing, and I'm trying to steer them back to the materials. We keep getting into little conversations that I get involved with in order to connect with them (and because their interests are surprisingly similar to mine in many respects), but when I try to get back on track, they get off on another tangent. We talk about Sega (which I have), music (which we don't have very much in common), New York, where they've all spent some time, and a lot of jokes about why I want to be a teacher. Finally, I decide to try to spend some time questioning Bernaldo about more general things, and put the subject on the back burner. I find out that Bernaldo moved to this country about seven years ago, and that he spent the first five in New York (on the Lower East Side). He thinks school is pretty useless, but thinks Mr. McKnight is a pretty good teacher because at least he keeps you awake. He has no idea what he wants to do with his life, but knows he wants to make money. He has an older sister and a younger brother, and his parents are divorced. He lives with his mom (I tell him it's the same way with me growing up). His father is still in Puerto Rico and he sees him occasionally, but he's spent a lot more time with his cousins in New York. There's no group work in this class, so I don't get any ideas about how he works with groups in school, but these four are buddies and hang out a lot after school—mostly playing Sega or reading comic books (that's what I did a lot as an undergraduate in college!). He also plays a lot of basketball, but non-competitively, just shooting around with his friends. I wish I could ask him more about his classroom experiences and the "classroom society" but, if you haven't guessed by now, there just ain't much of one. I end off trying a few more times to get things back on track to the review, but the whole thing eventually kind of dribbles out and by that time class had ended. I told Mr. McKnight about what had happened and he said he wasn't too concerned that we hadn't done much review, a lot of that went on silently in his class anyway (the only time the classroom is quiet). In the end, I thank him and move on.

EVALUATION: What surprised me most was two things— Mr. McKnight's flawless ability to control the classroom without stifling participation, and the amount of participation that actually occurred, some at a very high level of thinking, in a low-track class. What surprised me most about Bernaldo, though in retrospect it shouldn't, is his complete lack of direction in life. I remember when I was sixteen, I already had the next ten years of my life pretty well conceived (though it turns out I was wrong about almost everything), but I guess a lot of that stems from the fact that I came from a privileged white background, and had a lot more options open to me. The other thing that surprised me, and in a very positive way, was the ease with which I was able to converse with Bernaldo and his friends, and their rather quick acceptance of me as someone they could talk to. It was also kinda funny to find out just how much we had in common as far as our outside activities, and could therefore connect on. Hey, just another example of how very different paths can lead to the same destination. I really don't know where Bernaldo might end up, but I think that he probably has a better chance than some of his background to make something of his life, in whatever area.

INTERVIEW WITH MR. MCKNIGHT: Mr. McKnight has been in education, as a teacher, coach, and administrator, for a long time and has quite a bit of practical experience at all levels. Nonetheless (or perhaps because of this) he is quite an iconoclast, and is very quick to voice his own opinions.

I asked him about parental involvement and whether it was the panacea some envision. He replied that, on the most recent parents' day, he only had about 30 parents show up, out of about 100+ kids he teaches, and that was the highest total in the department. Furthermore, most of the parents who did show up were from his highest-tracked class, and none showed up from his lowest-tracked class. But he doesn't think there's much of a correlation there, despite appearances, or at least not much of one that could be easily changed. While he does think that some things could be done to marginally increase parental involvement, for most of these kids, their parents wouldn't show up unless physically forced. Many of them work a second or third job in the evening, and do not have the time to take off to come to school, and many of the others aren't from this country and think that coming to your child's school is a bad thing. In addition, a lot of the rest had bad school experiences themselves and are either afraid of the school, or just don't put much emphasis on the importance of school. With these types of parents, he said, increasing parental involvement is unlikely, at best, and the efforts that would be needed to seriously increase it would be more trouble than they're worth. So while there might well be a correlation between parental school experience and involvement and student achievement, most of the numbers don't lend themselves to tinkering very much.

On the subject of multiculturalism and other programs he is even more opinionated. The first thing he does is go into a tirade about ESL and other bilingual programs. They take a tremendous amount of money, money that is in very short supply, and could be used more advantageously elsewhere. Furthermore, what really upsets him is that if a student comes in who speaks Polish or Russian or any of the other less popular languages, they put him or her into an ESL class for Spanish or Portuguese, and so the poor kid has to learn Spanish and English at the same time in order to have any hope of learning English. He thinks that foreign students should be placed in a total immersion program, which allows them to learn English as quickly as possible, and then put them in regular classrooms. In his own class, when faced with a student who doesn't yet have a great command of English, he puts them next to one of his better students, so that they might copy the other person's notes and ask for help as needed. But he really hates the amount of resources that go into special ed. programs.

The next subject of attack is the bureaucracy and the tremendous drain it also exerts on the school budget with very limited results. He thinks that teachers should control the classroom, and do whatever works best for them (he also hates teacher unions).

On the subject of other areas of multiculturalism, he just scoffs. First of all, there aren't the resources to implement a multicultural agenda even if there was one available. Second, he hasn't noticed the kind of cultural isolationism that many of the texts point to, and thinks that, in classes on an equal level, there is no gap between the achievement of white and non-white students. I think part of this stems from the fact that he is a popular teacher throughout the school, and makes sure that everyone participates to some degree. He's certainly one of the more successful ones, by most standards. The rest of the multicultural agenda he regards as neat academic ideas that have little life in the classroom. The text is pretty standard and there just isn't time to teach things that aren't there, or even all the things that are. Overall, coming from a successful classroom and with a lot of experience under his belt, I think that Mr. McKnight's opinions, while certainly out of the mainstream of thought today, certainly deserve some consideration, especially considering that most of our analyses have been structural and sociological, which suffer from the twin faults of being very slippery with the statistics (as do all of the "soft" sciences from psychology to economics) as well as depending on statistical norms as opposed to single classrooms. No, I don't think Mr. McKnight is entirely right, or even mostly right, but I do think that when the study of how a class operates becomes more important than the actual results of classroom achievement, we are stepping very close to the line of letting the cart drive the horse. I don't know, ask me in ten years, after I've actually been out there, and I'll be able to give you a more definitive answer.

Chapter Four

McKNIGHT IN ACTION: This is a story with a theme, specifically the economic conditions in the United States following World War I. It started with a single fact, that the period was marked by violent strikes, and used that single fact to construct a picture of the whole economy. So let's join our sleuths already in progress…

Ray "Sherlock" McKnight paced around the room like a caged animal. "All right, my young Watsons, just what are we dealing with here? No, no, don't look at your books, we're not going to solve this mystery by looking at the book, let's just see what was happening. Mr. Watson, what's something that characterized the period?"

Mr. Watson looked around desperately. Without the book to rely on he seemed a bit lost. "Well, there were lots of violent strikes…"

Sherlock jumped on that fact immediately, like a dog who had just found the scent of a rabbit. "Excellent. Now why? What was it about this period that would lead to such violent clashes? Miss Watson?"

Miss Watson was tentative in her reply. "Unemployment?"

A smile spread across Sherlock's face. "Good. There was

high unemployment. Now why was there such high unemployment. Was there a recession? What was going on? Yes, Watson."

This Watson seemed to be beginning to grasp what was going on. "The war had just ended."

Sherlock probed for more. "And…"

Watson made another effort. "And all the soldiers were coming home."

Sherlock was ecstatic. "Right. Suddenly there were four million young men coming back from Europe, and they all wanted to get back to their old lives, which meant that they needed jobs. So, why weren't there jobs to be had?"

A deathly silence fell across the class. No one seemed to want to offer a response.

Sherlock was undaunted. He tried another tack. "Well, there was no lack of jobs during the war, right? So why aren't there jobs for the returning soldiers?"

One Watson finally seemed to grasp what was going on. "There were no more jobs making things for the war."

Once more, Sherlock was ecstatic. "Exactly. The war industry shut down, and with it went a lot of jobs. So there was a lot of fear of unemployment. What did the soldiers do about it?"

No one volunteered, so Sherlock went on. "Does anyone remember the Bonus marches? What were they?"

A Watson piped up. "Soldiers wanting the government to give them money?"

Sherlock took that point and ran with it. "Right. Soldiers coming home wanted the government to make up for the wages they had lost fighting in Europe when they could have been working at home. They wanted the government to give them a nest egg. So what happened? Did they get it?"

One of the Watsons was ready. "No."

"And why not? It seems like the government would want to reward those kids who had fought and died for their country."

This time Miss Watson was less confident in her reply. "They didn't have the money?"

Sherlock smiled. "Exactly. The government had run up a big war debt during the conflict, and didn't want to raise taxes, so they had no money to give them. OK. Now what else was going on during this time that might lead to violent strikes? What was everyone afraid of?"

A word rang out from somewhere in the classroom. "Bolsheviks."

"Right. Who were the Bolsheviks?"

"Communists?"

"And what had they just done to make people so nervous?"

"Taken over Russia."

"Nice work, Mr. Watson," said Sherlock, shaking his hand. "Did everyone get that? The Bolsheviks had taken over Russia and now everyone thought that every worker strike was the beginning of a communist revolution here in the U.S. What do we call this fear?"

A few voices spoke up together. "Red scare."

"Right, and was it true? Were we ever in danger of being taken over by Bolsheviks?"

This time nearly everyone joined in. "No."

"Exactly. It was just a paranoid reaction to what had happened to Russia. OK, one more piece to the puzzle. What about immigration? Was it rising or falling?"

Someone spoke up. "Rising."

"Right. Now what about these immigrants. Did they join

unions? Did they get jobs right away?"

One Watson was ready. "No, they just took work wherever they could get it."

"And what kind of work was easily available to them?"

Watson knew where this was headed. "Work replacing striking workers."

Sherlock laughed. "Exactly. Immigrant scabs. So what happened? Were the American people happy about this?"

"No."

"And what did the government do about it? Mr. Watson?"

"They stopped letting people in."

Sherlock developed the point. "Or at least they clamped down on it to slow down the number of people coming in. Right. What about the people themselves? What group made a revival during this time?"

This one went over everyone's head. "What group? They were big in the south during reconstruction. Wore white."

By now one Watson had figured it out. "The KKK?"

"Exactly. There was a KKK revival during the early twenties. And they weren't just going after Blacks now, they were going after immigrants. OK. So, there it is, the situation after World War I. Just remember—none of these things were going on in a vacuum. All this stuff is connected. So, when you're studying for the test keep that in mind. Don't just memorize names and dates. This is the real world. Right? So look at all the stuff and try to see how it fits together. I guarantee it does, because it all happened. Remember, this is history. We're talking about things that happened. So look for the connections."

And they moved on to another mystery.

So, there you have it. A class about a theme—the post-war economy. You can see how Mr. McKnight took what the students knew and developed it into a coherent picture of the country at the time, relying mostly on input from the students, but putting it in a larger context. I think that's why the class works. He keeps the students alert and involved by using their knowledge, but manages to gather it together thematically in a way most of these kids haven't grasped yet. I think it works.

RAY McKNIGHT: Ray McKnight is a little unusual in appearance. He has a big, bushy, handlebar mustache, and he smiles a lot. So, at first glance, one might not be inclined to take him seriously. But once he opens up his mouth, you can't help but listen. I think one of his strongest aspects as a teacher is his attitude towards the material. He honestly believes that history is fun, interesting, and most importantly, relevant to the kinds of things we're dealing with today, and his students might be dealing with tomorrow. He makes this very clear in his presentations—constantly making contemporary references, using analogies that compare history to today's headlines. He's also trying very hard to pound into these kids' heads that history isn't a series of disconnected facts; rather it is one continuous stream of events, each linked to the earlier ones, and that together they make up a coherent picture of where we came from. His style can't help but be participatory. He checks homework every day, outlines what the students should write in their notes, and is constantly calling on students to make a point, which he then expands on. He also uses a great deal of positive reinforcement—both verbal and physical (his patented handshakes) and, even if the students think it is corny, you can tell they appreciate it. He obviously likes what he's doing, and some of that enthusiasm can't help but rub off on his students.

I think that the students are, in fact, buying it. This is a class of generally uninspired students, and yet their response to him is quite exceptional. There is quite a lot of student participation in class, even if most conversations are two ways, between him and the students, rather than between the students, and the students are obviously pleased by his praise of them. He has such a good rapport with them that I have never seen a discipline problem in his class (part of that might be due to the fact that he is so loud that no one else can talk unless he lets them). I also think they like that he doesn't try to make them do more than they're ready to give. If they offer an answer to his question, even if that answer is largely irrelevant or inadequate he'll use what they say as a springboard to where he wants to go. His constant movement around the room and enthusiasm makes it impossible to be too distracted by anything else and, at the same time, I don't think there's even a covert effort on the part of the students to escape the process—they let him in and he's glad to be there.

I don't think the students pick up much that isn't right there for all to see. They might observe his easy rapport with the kids, the enthusiasm he has for the subject and the learning process, and the way students respond to it. And they might get the sense that he really cares about the students and works hard to help them "get it". Other than that, there's not much subtlety in Mr. McKnight's presentations, it's all right there.

What I really got is a sense of just how important positive reinforcement is, especially for kids this age. If you asked them outright whether or not they care if a teacher shows approval most would probably deny it, but there's no way to hide the pride that these kids exhibit when he remarks that their answer was "excellent" or, even better, shakes their hand. They just seem to straighten up in their chairs when such things happen, and I noticed that kids he heaped these praises on were more likely to respond to questions later than they were before he singled them out. I guess that 16-17 year olds are so unsure about their own identity and self-worth that praise from a teacher whom they all obviously respect can help them a lot.

But what stands out the most for me is the way McKnight manages to keep everyone involved in the learning process, especially those who aren't on a college track. Maybe most teachers manage to do this today, but, from my own remembrances of high school, I can only remember a few teachers who managed to keep everyone's attention as well as this. The kids feel comfortable in his class, and I can't say enough about how this feeling helps in the students' learning.

Chapter Five

Note: Stephen wrote the following paper for his graduate school class on Teacher Observation, summarizing the influence of Mr. McKnight.

If You Want to Fly, You Have to Think Like a Bird
Or
Teacher-Student/Student-Teacher

One thing in particular that I have found common to all the great teachers I have observed is a real connection to the students—who they are, where they come from, and what they do outside of school. It seems to me that it is only through this type of connection, seldom mentioned in education courses, that teachers are able to forge the type of bond that gives teachers what they need most—the trust and respect of their students. Kids of 16, 17, or 18 are, for the most part, insecure, unsure, and often confused about their lives and where they are heading, and so it takes someone they can trust to make them open up—both emotionally and intellectually. Why? Because in order to learn something, really LEARN it, you have to care about it, you have to think it is important, and you have to be willing to work for it. For some students, this is easy: they are self-mo-tivated, know where they are going, and are able to connect schoolwork with these goals in such a way as to make it important to them. But, as I mentioned above, this is not the case for most students. They need something else, and that something else can only be supplied by the teacher. A good teacher is able to make them care about the subject because, in some sense, they know that he or she cares about them, and there-fore would not try to teach them something that was of no use, and it is because of this assumption that the students try to find for themselves the value of learning. Maybe this is not the only way to become a good teacher. Spectacular presentations and overwhelming charisma also spring to mind, but it seems to me to be one of the most effective. I observed just such a teacher as part of my fieldwork.

One way of showing this connection, this caring, that I have seen repeatedly, and which seems to work remarkably well, is a connec-tion to school sports. It's become almost a cliché in America, the idea of a basketball or football coach who also teaches history or civics, and I, like many others I know, have often scoffed at the idea, feeling that it cheapens the value of teaching history, but multiple observations have changed my mind dramatically about this. Teachers who are also coaches have two big advantages over their colleagues—first, because school sports are so important to many communities, a connection with them shows school spirit, enthusiasm, and a willingness to share time that is not required in the job description. It also lets the teacher get to know lots of kids outside of the classroom environment, in a setting in which they are more likely to be themselves. The other great advantage is that coaches must know something about motivation—about getting kids to care and work when it just doesn't seem to be worth it anymore. Furthermore, as a coach, a teacher has to learn to give up some aspect of control. He can teach and drill and plan all he wants, but once the game starts, it's all in the hands of the players. I think that this attitude helps teachers to remember that it is the students, not the teachers, who are at the center of the classroom experience, and that what the teacher accomplishes is nothing compared to what the kids accomplish.

For these reasons, I was particularly interested in the interactions that took place, both in the halls and in the classroom, related to school sports. This was the end of the basketball season, and the school had done very well—was, in fact, preparing for the state championship tournament—and you could see the bond, the enthusiasm, between the teacher and students whenever the subject of basketball was brought up. Both the kids and the teacher seemed to be at ease in these conversations, and they seemed to interact on a much more human level than the typical student/teacher conversations. For this reason, I found them to be profoundly important to the teaching experience, and a large part of what makes this teacher so good.

Another topic, quite similar in some ways, is work. At many schools, especially in the lower economic stratums, many kids have after-school jobs, and these jobs become very important to the kids—both as a source of income, and as a tool of self-expression and worth. When teachers take the time to find out about these jobs, either by asking the kids or seeing them outside the classroom, it helps form the same kind of bond I mentioned above. It shows the kids that they exist for the teacher outside of the classroom experience, and that the teacher, at some level, understands what's going on in their lives apart from schoolwork. In addition, it helps boost self-esteem by letting the students and teachers interact, not as a superior to a subordinate, but as one working person to another. Just such an interaction took place while I was there, and you could see the kid sit up straighter in the seat, talk openly about the lousy working conditions and, in general, really connect with the teacher.

On the question of a negative interaction, I will turn to myself to point out a case where the interaction was not so much negative, but unsuccessful. One thing that I picked up as part of my classroom experience was a profound sense that students have very little idea about the logic by which the outside world operates, especially in its more abstract forms. This is certainly understandable, as they generally have very little chance to operate in the circles in which such decisions are made, and it is only recently that I myself have begun to acquire some confidence that my own reading of the world reflects, at least on some level, reality, but for students it is one big black hole. This came to the fore most clearly when, during my first week of teaching, while making my presentation on credit cards, I was struck by the silence whenever I asked the question, "Why do you think that the company wants to know that?" or "Why do you think that they made that decision?" I can't remember a single case when I got a response to that type of question, and no wonder— why should they know it? Later on, during the second week, when they were making those decisions for themselves, I found that they had indeed come up with answers to some of those questions, but it was in the context of constructing their own logical model, not trying to fathom the depths of the existing corporate one. The best example of this is when they decided that, as part of the application, the company could ask the applicant if they had ever been convicted of a white-collar crime, but were excluded from asking about any other, such as burglary, robbery, or murder. The logic: a person convicted of a white-collar crime has exhibited behavior that might cause concern to a credit card company—fraud or embezzlement—and this might affect the likelihood that they will pay their debts, whereas other types of crime, while morally reprehensible, have nothing to do with billing or payment, and should therefore be excluded. In other words, when the students were thinking on their own, for themselves, and against no predetermined set of "right" answers, they were more confident and willing to express themselves, whereas when asked to try to figure out a part of the world of which they had no knowledge, their self-consciousness took over and they clammed up.

I guess the lesson that comes out of all of this is the idea that, in order to be an effective teacher, you have to be willing to make the effort to enter into the students' world, while not expecting them to be so willing, or able, to fully enter your own. Again, it comes back to the idea that the classroom is a place designed to serve the student, and the teacher's job is to transform themselves in such a way as to do that effectively, regardless of what they might think or been taught prior to entering the classroom. A religious cynic (I forget who) once played off the old Biblical phrase "God created man in his own image" by rewriting it as "Man created God in his own image." Teachers should, with all sincerity, be willing to do the same. The old paradigm that "Teachers create students in their own image" must be reversed to "Students create teachers in their own image." Of course, this is much easier said than done, but, in the end, it might prove a key in making education in our society effective on into the future.

PART THREE
Fall 1994: Practice Teaching

"The Therasan begin adopting individual names to express this new freedom and name themselves after their proudest achievement. The Ceremony of Naming, held when each individual feels that they have done something worthy of naming, becomes an important part of each Therasan's life and central to their social interaction. But the Therasan demand more. They desire to express their perspective in a concrete manner. Saren teaches them numbers and geometry so that they might create monuments to their individuality."

—*The History of Lathrim*

Chapter One

ARMINGTON STREET PROVIDENCE

August 31: Well, here I am, the day before I start teaching. It's 4:45 in the morning, and I have to be at work in 3 hours 15 minutes. If you haven't already guessed, I'm pulling an all-nighter. Some of my earlier fears have been laid to rest after another meeting with Ms. Hill. She seems willing to give me lots of control over the classroom, maybe TOO much control, as it's been hinted that she won't even be there while I'm teaching. At least she's letting me go forward with my lesson plans, from the "What good is history?" writing assignment to the "kill a mastodon experiment." Her only advice is to have lots of backup material ready in case any or all of this blows up in my face. That's reassuring. I really want to prove her wrong, prove that I can get through to the kids enough to engage them on the issues of history, to get them thinking about the issues of various people, something she doesn't seem to think is possible, but maybe that's all just youthful idealism. I sure hope not, otherwise it's going to be a long painful career. I guess my biggest fear right now (apart from outright humiliation) is that I only do so-so. It's just like with standardized tests—I expect, at least in my own heart, to do fantastic, so even an above-average result is something of a disappointment. The same goes here. I know that I can explain history better than just about anyone I know, that I can make it interesting, that I care about learning. But will that be enough, at least at the start? I don't know. At least I know that there are a lot of people far worse prepared than I, doing the exact same thing, and they seem to get along OK, so perhaps my fears are unfounded. I hope so.

Monday, September 5: Well, I think it's the 5th. In any case, it's Labor Day (or at least it was until 4½ hours ago) and I have school in 3½ hours. I have just finished reading the essays that I had the kids write on Friday, so here are some initial impressions. First, I shouldn't have told the B levels that I only wanted half a page, because that's the most I got. I thought that a full page would intimidate them (especially after my Freshman A's complained), but in retrospect, I should have gone for the full page, at least I would have gotten something more out of them (though their results are not a complete disappointment). Second, I think it is interesting that I got far more positive responses out of the second and third classes I posed this question to than from the group I first tried it on. I think it has something to do with the fact that after my first class I was better prepared to present the case for history, whereas the first time around I was just winging it. Chalk up another source for preparation. You just can't say enough good things about it. Now, on to content. What struck me most was the fact, for the most part, these kids are **HORRIBLE** writers. I can't even begin to run down the list of problems they had with a simple one-page essay, from grammar to sentence structure to spelling. It's going to take a **HELL** of a lot of work to get even a marginally good paper out of them (this includes the A's). Well, everyone says I'm a great writer and a potentially great teacher, so I guess this is my first chance to prove it. By the end of the semester I want at least one 3 to 5-page paper out of each of these kids. That's my goal. Let's see if I can do it. However, all that aside, there was some hope to be found in the content. A lot of these kids aren't dumb (in all of the classes), they've just been taught badly up to now. I can't imagine how they got into high school writing this badly. But they've shown me that they have something to work with, so that's what I'm gonna have to do.

Tuesday, September 6: Well, here I am, just about 24 hours later than the last entry, and as you can probably tell, my sleeping schedule is still way off. Oh well, I'll get it right soon enough. Let's see. You know, today, for the first time, I really felt comfortable teaching. It's funny, because I know that feeling is false—it will be a long time before I have any right to feel confident and comfortable going into any classroom situation, a fact that became obvious later on in the day. But let's try to clarify things. First of all, I think that the worksheets I made after writing last night's journal entry turned out great. They test the things I went over; they start out easy and get harder, and there's enough of a friendly feel to them that they're not entirely sterile. And by the same token, the prepared lesson I came up with seemed good too, getting the points about different books, and how to use them in such a way as to familiarize the kids with the materials. So I went to school feeling that I was prepared.

There is a balance between teaching that requires just rote reaction, and teaching that requires real thinking, and I think

I leaned too heavily in the former direction. However, maybe that's not such a bad thing; because I did make sure that I got an answer from just about everyone in the class (even those who didn't want to answer). Lack of interaction and response is one of my biggest fears as a teacher, so maybe, by giving them easy answers to give now, they might be more willing to respond later. I'll have to see how it goes. When I got to the worksheet there was a problem. The problem is that these kids aren't very good readers (I heard that most of them read at about a fourth grade level), and the book's awfully difficult. Part of the goal of this lesson was to familiarize the kids with the book so that it doesn't seem so intimidating, but maybe these kids have some reason to feel intimidated. Anyway, the lecture part of the lesson went on longer than I thought and so there was only about 10 minutes left at the end of class to start on it. I'm planning to spend the whole of today's class working with the kids, so we'll see how they respond. I must say that in the few minutes they were working on it they made some mistakes that I hadn't even imagined were possible. I don't want to make this sound like a disaster in the making, but I can tell right now that I'm going to have trouble with the B's. There are some real smart-asses in the class but, unfortunately, they're also the smartest kids (or at least the ones most willing to respond to questions) so finding the right way to handle them will be a problem.

Anyway, I had some difficulty dealing with the class. Not a lot, but enough to remind me I'm still real green. Most troubling is I was beginning to get the first whiffs of a class that was getting out of hand, something I'm oversensitive to because of my real discomfort with discipline. The way I tried to handle it was through ignoring the obvious attempts to get a rise out of me, and rolling with the punches on the rest, trying to ride the wave, so to speak. The problem with that approach is that I did nothing to stem the upward flow, so either they're going to get tired of it and like me enough to settle down some, or they're going to keep testing me, to the point where I have no choice but to respond. I hope it doesn't come to that, but it very well might at some point.

Thursday, September 8: All right, I'm a little discouraged. I gave the first part of my lecture on capitalism to my B's, the first time I had really lectured to them since the first day, and something didn't click. Ms. Hill told me that capitalism was a hard topic to teach these kids, but I guess, in my arrogance, I was counting on my ability to explain things clearly (one of the talents I had always thought would make me a good teacher) to carry the day. Well, it didn't. I mean it wasn't a complete disaster, and I got out the information that I wanted to, but I don't think that I reached anyone on a basic level, something I really hoped to do during this talk.

Part of the reason might be I hadn't prepared as fully as I wanted. I guess I slacked off a bit last night, and was counting on this morning and early afternoon to give me the time to prepare what I needed to talk about, but as often is the case, when I actually got to school, there were several distractions that kept me from devoting the time I wanted to preparing the lecture. I mean I had time to reread the chapter, and put together my notes, but there wasn't enough left to really come up with an overall strategy that might have made this lecture more successful and comprehensive. Also, there wasn't the kind of response from the class, the kind of interaction I was hoping for that might have given me the feedback to tell me whether or not this stuff was getting across. I tried to use examples that would mean something to the kids, such as using the invention of a motorized sneaker to demonstrate the way supply and demand work together in the market to determine prices, but I think that was more distracting than useful. By the end, I was so desperate to get the kids involved that, when I asked for another example to show the way a product comes to market, and one of the kids laughingly suggested stainless steel condoms, I decided to go with it, and followed the development of stainless steel condoms from conception to manufacture to distribution. Somehow I don't think that that episode won me any respect in the class.

Sunday, September 11: Well, I'm sick. I've been running a low-grade fever all weekend, and I can't stop sneezing. I **REALLY** want to go in tomorrow, and I thought I'd be able to (at least for the first three periods that I teach), but I've been sitting here updating this journal and the effort has made me realize just how weak I am. Considering the fact that I'm planning (by coincidence) to lecture to all three classes tomorrow, I don't think I'll be able to make it. On the one hand, I feel like I'm giving up too early, not putting up the good fight, especially this early in the year, but the worst possible thing would be for me to go in tomorrow and then collapse, having to miss even more days. But, dammit, I'm **DEFINITELY** going in Tuesday. Oh, well, at least I'll have a chance to catch up on my paperwork.

You know, it's kind of weird. Normally I'm something of a slacker and will take any opportunity to take a day off from work (or school). But now I'm pissed that I'm going to miss a day. Someone else will be lecturing to my kids, **AND**

TEACHING THEM WRONG. It's like loaning the keys to your Ferrari to a friend—you just don't want to part with them, even for a day, because you don't know what'll happen. I'm especially worried about my A's. I'm right in the middle of a carefully planned set of lessons, and I don't know what to tell Ms. McVeigh to do in my absence. I just hope she doesn't mess up and make my job harder when I get back. I'm less worried about Ms. Hill. In fact, it might help me by showing the kids just how lucky they are to have me and not her. Maybe they'll appreciate me more, and it'll definitely give more credibility to my threat to send them over to her.

Note: I forgot to put something important in my journal entry for Thursday. On Thursday I executed my first act of discipline. There were two kids in my B class (two fairly bright kids) who just wouldn't sit down and listen. Finally, after giving them several warnings, I marched them over to Ms. Hill in the History Office. Well, Ms. Hill played the part like an angry priest, and I think the kids were both ashamed of themselves, and afraid of her. On Friday, when I threatened to do the same thing again, the kids settled down right away. I hate to say it, but I'm coming around to her view. Some kids are just going to test you, test your limits, and won't stop until you give them a good quick kick in the butt (figuratively speaking). I thought that kindness and enthusiasm could win over anyone (it has in work experiences), but school is a whole other ball game, and sometimes you have to put your foot down. Thank God I have Ms. Hill to play the heavy for me (as I'm really bad at confrontation), but I'll eventually have to do it myself. I'm surprised that it came to this, but I really don't think you can have control over the classroom (in a positive sense) until the kids realize what the limits are. In fact, I've been so unsure of my control level that I've delayed using any cooperative activities for fear of losing the little control I had. Maybe now these sorts of things will be more possible. I'm shocked that I've reached this conclusion so fast, but, as I'm so quick to quote, book knowledge and theory is no substitute for experience. Score one for their side.

Wednesday, September 14: OK, today was something of a trial (but that doesn't mean it was all bad). Let's see…First class today was my B level. This turned out to be a disaster, not in the sense that the class got out of control or anything, but just in the sense that I failed to accomplish what I wanted. It was a classic case of Greek hubris. What I intended to do (despite warnings from Ms. Hill that it wouldn't work) was teach them most of the rest of the capitalism lesson, including corporate structures, changes in the US economy in the years following the Civil War, and the business cycle. Even typing it up here I can see that it was an outrageous agenda, but at the time it seemed so interconnected that if I didn't get it all done at once, none of it would make sense. And, try as I might, I just couldn't get anything to stick. In the end, it turned out to be not only frustrating for me, but I'm sure it was tremendously frustrating for them, and I think I did them a disservice by trying to force it down their throats. Very little was accomplished. I guess tomorrow I'm going to have to go and try to salvage what I can out of the lesson, picking up the pieces, so to speak. I might even try to start the whole thing over again, and just go into the ideas at a basic level, minus all the bells and whistles. Whatever I do, I hope I haven't done anything that's going to hurt my relationship with these kids permanently, since it is these kids more than any others that I want to help. OK, got that out of my system, on to other things.

My A level class was the last period. First thing I noticed was that they were anxious to play my *Jeopardy!* game—a good sign. But, because it was last period and I wanted to get <u>some</u> work done, I decided to spend the first 20 minutes of class lecturing, and then move onto the game. This had more or less mixed results. First of all, the lecturing part went well—I went back over the Australopithecus and Homo habilis stuff, and moved a little more ahead, setting up for more lecturing later. You know, I hate to admit it (or maybe I don't) but it's so much more pleasurable to lecture to A's than other groups! They ask better questions, they raise interesting points, they make perceptive comments. The whole package. It brings up the dilemma I'm wrestling with overall with regard to my teaching career—I could go and find some nice suburban school and teach kids like this happily for the rest of my life, but I know that it isn't these kids that need the most help, and the place I might be able to do the most good is in an inner city or urban environment. I don't know what direction I'll end up going, but I'm rapidly approaching a crossroads at which I'll have to deal with it. For the game, I used the classic *Jeopardy* method—that is, I divided the class into two teams (the Aces and the Hot Dogs as it turned out) and asked each team a question in turn. If they got it right, they got points. If they got it wrong, the other team got a chance to answer and steal the points. Whichever team ended up winning I told them I'd bump them up a third of a grade on the test. And you know, for an oldie it sure worked. We had questions flying, answers flying, all sorts of things flying everywhere, and I even managed to step in occasionally to explain what a particular answer meant. I'm not sure everyone got everything, but it sure worked better than anything else I could have possibly come up with. Let's hope they're ready for the test tomorrow! Anyway, the game itself took up most of the class. Oh well, it's my own damn fault. I'm actually lucky because Ms. McVeigh doesn't care what pace we proceed at in the class—a good thing since we're two weeks into school and I'm still at Homo habilis. But at some point I'm going to have to speed things up. We'll see.

Thursday, September 15, 1994: Well, I have my first official test today as a teacher. I had two real concerns about it—time and difficulty, one of which proved unfounded, the other I'm not sure. The concern I had with time proved unnecessary— the kids managed to finish with plenty of time left, although I don't know if that means they thought it was easy, or if they just left a lot of things blank. We'll see. Ms. Hill thought it was a good test, so that's a good sign, but I'm still not sure if it wasn't above their level. I know there are no surprises on it, everything there we went over at least twice, usually three times and, since it was open-book, there's no reason they shouldn't be able to get it, but maybe I'm just overconfident. My A's went fine too. The class got a little out of hand yesterday because I realized that the only way to do the game right was to go to each kid individually, and so the rest of the class had nothing to do, but I solved that problem by putting together two readings for them, from Everyday Life through the Ages and Ideas That Changed the World, and gave them a worksheet based on them. In total there was only sixteen pages of reading, and lots of pictures in there, but Ms. McVeigh seemed to think it was a lot, and I guess it was, considering the entire book chapter on this era is only eight pages itself. Oh, well, that just goes to show how woefully inadequate the book is in covering this critical area of human history.

Friday, September 16, 1994: Well, I haven't looked at the tests yet, so I'm still in a good mood. I decided not to start a new chapter with my A's, so I did a current events class on Haiti, since invasion seems imminent. I wanted to spend a lot of time with their own ideas about the invasion—whether it was a good idea, what it was about, why we're doing it, etc., but what I found is that they knew nothing whatsoever about it, so the class turned more into a lecture about the history of Haiti and US involvement than anything else. It was only in the last ten minutes or so that they began expressing their opinions about it (generally along the lines that it was a bad idea and if Clinton was so in favor of it he should lead the troops himself). I'm appalled at their total ignorance of current events, although I suppose I shouldn't be. I think I'll be doing more of these current events classes in the future. With my A's I decided to try to move ahead with the lectures on early man, as I'll have to get to a test next week (and Ms. Hill is already starting Sumeria). We moved from Homo habilus to Homo erectus, his spread around the world, and then I was just getting to the emergence of Homo sapiens and the contrast with Neanderthal when class ended. I hope they're getting it. The rest of the time I spent trying to explain the ideas of Darwinism and Social Darwinism, and who might be in favor of them and why. Not a lot of feedback, so I don't know if it got through. Damn!

Monday, September 19, 1994: Well, I got the tests graded… On the whole they were not good. The highest raw score was an 83 (out of 110 including bonus points). Most of them did well on the table, and I got some other scattered good answers, but there were two main problems. First was the section on the business cycle. I thought it was an easy way to get points because they just had to put the steps in the cycle into the right order, which should have been easy considering I put them all up onto the board last week, but this proved not to be the case. I don't know what was going through some of their minds as they arranged these steps, but some of the orderings were truly bizarre. Most of them lost at least ten points on this section (one kid, Cathy, got the whole thing right, but she was the only one) and many lost fifteen or more. The other area they messed up was the differences between a private and public company, again a section I thought would be easy but which proved to be no such thing. Oh, well. What I decided to do is spend the class going over the test, and give the kids the chance to earn extra points (up to twenty) by correcting their mistakes and turning it back in. I made a list of which kids did well on which questions, and so when I called on kids to give me the answers to the questions I knew I was calling on someone who had the right answers, which might up the class participation rate overall. I was willing to give them until tomorrow to turn the test back in but, true to form, they didn't want to take it home, so they did the corrections while we were going over it, and they all gave it to me at the end of the class. The result is a respectable bell curve of scores (well, it was before too, but now it moves into the normal range). I was quite disappointed with the results, but Ms. Hill wasn't surprised at all. In fact, she seemed surprised that kids in a B-General did as well on this test as they did. She approved wholeheartedly of my resolution of the problem, and said to move on, which I'll do tomorrow. In my A's, I continued moving forward today, covering the time from the Neanderthal to the beginnings of farming. I spent a lot of time covering the reasons why Homo sapiens replaced Neanderthals, through out-breeding, and I think they got it, but I'm not 100% sure. I thought I'd be able to finish today, but I didn't get to domestication or metallurgy, since we ended up spending much more time on ancient religion than I had intended. The kids seemed really into it, so I decided to go with it. I'll finish up tomorrow and we'll have the test on Friday.

Tuesday, September 20, 1994: I'm pissed!@!!@##!#! I'm so goddamn fucking pissed!!!!!! I could eat concrete right now I'm so mad!!!!!! OK, take a breath...Ms. McVeigh dropped me from my World History class!!!!! GODDAMN IT! OK, let me start from the beginning. I talked to Ms. McVeigh after class last Thursday about the slow pace of the class and that I hoped it wasn't a problem. She told me it was fine, and her only concern was that there be enough grades in the book by the time warning cards came out. I told her that I'd have a test this week, along with the paper stemming from the game, and three worksheets, plus the book work she had them do the day I was sick, and that we'd soon be moving on to Sumeria. She said that was fine, and I thought that everything was OK. BUT, BUT, BUT...

Today after school she and the Principal, Dr. Laffey, (what he was doing there I don't know) had a talk with me in the history office, and she said that she wanted to take the class back for a month or so, and that maybe I could take it back again after that. I took the whole thing very calmly and asked *Why*? She then began stating a litany of problems she had with what I was doing, some of which I agreed with, some not. To wit: First, that I wasn't giving

enough homework assignments. She said that they should have homework every day and I wasn't giving it. (My answer—OK, I guess I wasn't giving that much homework, but since the class was built around my lectures, since the book covers this material so poorly, there wasn't a lot I could give. Besides, I wasn't giving any homework in my other classes [on the advice of Ms. Hill] so I thought that giving any homework at all was a step up. Also, she had never told me this was a problem before, ever.) Second, that the class was disruptive, and that the kids were getting out of hand. (My answer: I agreed the kids were sometimes loud, but that's how I wanted it to be, as long as it was a productive loud. I totally agree that last Wednesday when I went around the class doing the game, and the kids had nothing to do, they got way out of hand, but that's why on Thursday I gave them readings and a worksheet when I finished going around and doing the game, and Thursday was a lot better. I also think that it's hard for me to effectively run the class when she's been sitting in there from day one, and the kids aren't sure who's in charge.) Third, that we weren't moving fast enough. (I thought we'd already covered this.) Fourth, that I didn't come to her and go over what I was doing in the class enough, something that she related to the fact that my primary cooperative teacher was Ms. Hill and that they had different styles. (My side: I agreed I didn't come to her very often, but that was because she told me at the beginning I had carte blanche to teach the way I saw fit, and that, since I knew the subject better than she did anyway, she'd have a chance to learn it from me [her words, not mine]. Maybe I could have collaborated with her more often, but she never seemed interested in doing so.) Fifth, that I wasn't supposed to be teaching three classes from the start anyway, and that the experience might have overwhelmed me. (My side: Half true—I was making some of the same mistakes in all of my classes, something that might have been avoided if I had taken them on more gradually, but as far as keeping up on the materials, I'm already planning the stuff on Sumeria, so with regard to that I'm way ahead.) So she said she was taking over. (The whole time Dr. Laffey just sat there agreeing with her, despite the fact that he's never been in any of my classrooms and has no idea what's going on. I think he was just there for her moral support.)

Now, I just want to say that the rebuttals above were not my answers to her with regard to the problems she raised; THEY'RE ONLY MY ANSWERS TO MYSELF. In fact, I think I handled the whole thing remarkably calmly, listening intently, agreeing with what they said, saying I understood, and, in the end, taking it all without reply, BUT DAMN IT I'M PISSED!!! Why didn't she say anything on Thursday when I asked her how I was doing??? Why didn't she come to me—EVER—and state her concerns? NOOOOO... she just saves them all up, stuffs them into a sack, and hits me upside the head with them. That's the part that hurts most...the unexpectedness of the whole thing. I thought my A class was the best of them all, and I didn't see this coming from a mile away. I still have no real idea what happened. I don't know, maybe when I calm down there'll be some hope. But, in the meantime, DAMN!!! DAMN!!! DAMN!!!

Friday, September 23, 1994: Well, there is some joy in Mudville. Before I get to anything else, I have something to announce. I went to Ms. McVeigh after school today and humbly asked if there was any way I could be allowed to keep my class. We had a long (much longer than I intended—about an hour and a half) talk, in which she started out by saying *Yes*, and then we went on to talk about her concerns and how I could address them. I agreed with everything she said (even the dumb things) and made helpful and deferential statements along the way. I was just happy that she was letting me keep my favorite class! She seemed very friendly and nice, and I'm glad that we managed to work things out since, in all honesty, I had never really seen what the problem was in the first place. Oh, well, such is the life of a teacher. On to events.

With my B's I started doing another current events lesson—this one on Bosnia. Again I wanted their feelings about it, but again I was shocked and appalled at their ignorance. Most of them had never heard of Bosnia and none of them could show it to me on the map. So again I ended up doing a lot of talking about the history of Bosnia, the sides involved, and the reasons we're there. These kids are going to be voting soon, and it makes me shudder. At the end of class, I gave a quick quiz on the chapter—four quick sections—three on the inventions we had covered, and one on why we're in Haiti (they'd wanted to know if Haiti was going to be on a test and, in exasperation, I'd said *Yes*—so here it was).

My A's took the Early Man test; again I was afraid about the length and content, and again length didn't seem to be a problem, but I'm not sure about content. I know this was a hard test, but there was nothing there we hadn't covered repeatedly. Besides, these are A kids, they're supposed to be able to do better, so I'll see. With my two B classes the results were quite bizarre. They worked out to be a reverse bell curve! I had three kids who did very well—high 80s or 90s, one kid who did fine—70s, and three kids who did really badly—40s and 50s. One of these fails I can't explain—Arlindo, the brightest kid in the class. He did very well on most of the test, in fact he turned it in with a half-hour to go in class, but he didn't fill in one box on the first question—an easy section that everyone else got at least some points for, and which was worth 36 points. If he'd done that section he'd have gotten a 90, but because he didn't he ended up with a 56. I asked him why he hadn't filled anything in, and he just said he didn't have that stuff in his notebook, which was no answer because I know he knew the stuff—he'd gotten it right on the practice test, after all. I have yet to figure Arlindo out—he's really bright, and yet he's one of the biggest discipline problems left in the class, and he's always anxious to put me down. I'll have to spend some time trying to understand him—since he has more potential than any of my students, at any level.

Monday, September, 26, 1994: I have no idea what happened, but Ms. McVeigh took my World History class away from me again for good. I still have my regular history two classes.

Tuesday, September 27, 1994: Sorry about yesterday, but I was just stunned. I'll start again. I went to Ms. McVeigh before school about the tests (more on them later) to ask how she wanted me to handle them, and before I could say anything she informed me that she didn't want to do the split (splitting me with Ms. Hill) anymore, and that she was taking over the class. I have no idea why, since I had every reason to believe that we had worked things out Friday, but I have a few theories. First, the reasons she stated last Tuesday. I don't think any of them are big enough to take the class back, especially since I said I would change to suit her feelings, but maybe they were bigger than I suppose. But I don't think so, so from now on I'm going to engage in pure speculation, and I hope none of this sounds too petty...

First theory: I think I intimidate her with how much I know about the subject. She alluded to this on Friday when she said that one of the reasons she wanted me to use the book more was that when she took over the class after Christmas, that was all the kids would have, and that she didn't want them to get out of the habit of using it. I know that she has never taught this class at a high school level and that she doesn't know that much about it, so maybe she was afraid that the kids wouldn't like using the book again after I'd spent so much time moving beyond it. But, if this is true, I don't feel bad about my methods because the book is woeful in its coverage. In this case I wish her luck, and pity the kids—they're in for a long, boring year. Second theory: She has some personal problem with Ms. Hill and I ended up in the middle. I don't have any idea if this is true, but they don't seem to talk much. Third and most speculative theory: This is one that never occurred to me, but my stepmother, who knew Ms. McVeigh fairly well from her own teaching days, suggested it, so I might as well include it.

Ms. McVeigh is a pretty strong Catholic, and what I was teaching the kids was pure evolutionary theory, even down to the Eve theory about common ancestry, and this might have offended her religious sensibilities. She gave me absolutely no indication that this was the case at any point, so I'm quite skeptical about it as an idea, but, on the other hand, if it is true it might very well be the kind of thing she wouldn't address openly, so the lack of evidence might be explained. In all actuality I have no idea, but at this point the whole thing has been such a roller coaster ride that I'm just too drained to pursue it any further and will just chalk it up to experience. I tried to find out from Ms. Hill what happened but she said she didn't know, and that her impression was that it was some kind of personality conflict, again something I had had no inkling of during the whole time I worked with Ms. McVeigh. Oh, well. Since I'll now need a new third class for credit I talked to Ms. Hill and she said that we'd begin working for me to take over her own World History course, which was the class I had originally wanted.

Friday, September 30: Well, that cinches it. I can't do this anymore. I don't mean teaching; I mean teaching the way I've been teaching this week. The quizzes were abysmal, truly abysmal. I don't think I've ever been more discouraged. They learned nothing from the book, absolutely nothing. (I'm sorry, they did learn Carnegie was in steel, Rockefeller was in oil, and Morgan owned banks. Big whoop.) More than half the class flunked each quiz, and I was being quite generous in my grading. I did do one thing to try to wake them up. I started off the class with another current event issue—the fact that the US might be going to war with New Zealand over the Dabo islands—one of the richest sources of uranium in the world. I spoon-fed it to them, detail by detail of the history of the region, exactly like I had the previous two current events, and they ate it up. And then I revealed the fact that it was a complete lie—a fabrication of my imagination completely contrary to the facts. The point, as I explained it, was that these kids, in a couple of years, are going to be eligible to vote, and that every politician out there is going to hand them a load of crap at least as big as the one I just did—and unless they are capable of thinking for themselves, of finding out things for themselves, of weighing the evidence for themselves, they're going to fall for it again and again—victims of their own ignorance. I think it was a good try on my part, but even that was less than a success—I think the majority of them were just confused or resentful I would throw that kind of thing at them. I just want to **WAKE THEM UP!** They've shown sparks, here and there, and I've got to find a way to ignite those sparks into fire. They don't care about History, they don't care about the world in general, but there has to be something they do care about, some hook I can hang my lessons on that will draw them in. I'm not sure what it is, but it's out there and, until I get some inkling of what it is, I don't think I'm going to be able to get much further. Damn, it's frustrating to have all this knowledge and not be able to share it. It's like I've landed in Pearl Harbor the day before it's bombed and can't get anyone to listen to me when I say the Japanese are coming.

Monday, October 3: Well, today was a good day. I've pretty much abandoned the methods I used last week, despite their being in favor with Ms. Hill. I had to solo with my new World History class today for the first time because Ms. Hill was sick today. I wasn't really prepared, as this was not something we had planned, but I read up on the chapter real quick and that, along with what I already knew, was enough to get us through the decline of Egypt, the social structure of Egyptian society, and their achievements in science. Damn, those kids were glad not to have Ms. Hill, even for one day. I never knew 12 kids could make so much noise as they did when they first heard that Ms. Hill wasn't in. One loud, earthshaking cheer, and then it was on to business as usual. These seem like a real nice bunch of kids. I hate to admit it, but I'm really anxious to get back to teaching a class full of bright kids again. Nothing is quite as stimulating as to teach kids who ask the types of questions that make you, as a teacher, stop and think before you can answer them. That's what teaching is all about—interacting on as close to an equal level as possible and helping each other move up to the next higher plane together. Teaching has to be a two-way street and, intellectually, that's easiest with the brightest kids.

Thursday, November 10, 1994: Well, another week comes to an end, early as usual. What can I say about today? Well, I took my World History students to the library to begin researching their new papers. Mr. Rioux gave them a lecture about how to do research in a library and then they got to work looking up sources. I'm hoping that the fact that I gave them totally free rein in choosing their topic (I'm less interested in what they're writing than in teaching them the correct way TO write) will make them a little more enthusiastic about this project, though I'm sure their enthusiasm will be somewhat dampened when they realize how much work they're going to be doing on it. Hopefully it will pick up again when they see the final product. At least for the time being they seem energetic about what they're doing. I'm just going to have to find a way to shape these feelings in a productive manner. My other two classes were something of a disappointment. I was going around checking their work and wondering why they're having so much trouble finding the answers when I realized something—they hadn't even read the chapter. They were trying to find the answers without having any basis to find them. On the one hand I guess I shouldn't be surprised, given their lack of enthusiasm for the material, but I thought I'd cured them of this particular shortcut back when I made them write paragraph summaries of every paragraph in the chapter. I guess they didn't quite learn. What amazes me is how hard they try, and how long they take, trying to find the answers without reading the chapter, when it would be so much easier and faster if they just read the chapter first! I know that the book is a bad one, in either version, but I had no idea that their antipathy to reading it ran this deep. I might very well have to give up on the book altogether and just give them the stuff myself from now on. I've been contemplating this type of action for some time, I just haven't implemented it because I didn't feel that I could do the material justice (plus it's an awful lot more work for me, I must admit). Well, I guess I'll just have to suck it in and do it, because using the book has reached the point of no return. There just has to be another way.

Monday, November 14, 1994: Well, back from the long weekend. You know, when I was a kid I loved this kind of schedule, with lots of days off all over the place, but now, as a teacher, it's driving me crazy. There is not a single week this month in which we have a full five days of school. Last week we only had three days, this week we have some teacher thing on Friday, giving us only four, and next week is Thanksgiving, so there are only three there. Furthermore, for some reason it's my A division that gets screwed the most (at least from my perspective). They've already missed one day because of an assembly, and they're going to miss next Wednesday as well because of a pep rally. How am I supposed to be an effective teacher when my kids are out of school so much?!?! Before now I had always been in favor of increasing the school year to 210 days, as it is in most of the world, but only as a theoretical matter. Now I feel that it is absolutely necessary if we want to give our kids the type of learning experience they'll need for the future. Anyway, enough ranting. Today is Video Day in all my classes. I'm showing the beginning of the film, "I Will Fight No More Forever" about Chief Joseph and the Nez Perce Indians. This is one chapter that virtually cries out for illustration and, while the film isn't great, it does a more than adequate job of showing the types of problems the Indians faced during the great westward expansion. I want to make this an active, rather than a passive learning experience, especially since it will probably take three days to get through the film, so I'm giving them a worksheet each day about the events covered that day. Hopefully, it will help keep them focused. My A class began watching one of the new films the library got on ancient Greece, this one should give them some background on the art and philosophy of the period. I've watched it myself, and found it to be adequate, although far from great. I can't believe how much the library spent on these films! If this is how much it costs ($450 for four films) to increase the multimedia areas of school libraries, I now understand why they are growing so slowly. You'd think that the distributors would give libraries a break on prices for these things, but I guess, since libraries are their major market, they can't. I'm not saying that I know what the answer is, but I feel a hell of a lot less guilty about pirating some of this stuff, both for myself and for the school, now that I know how much it costs to buy. Oh, I also collected the paper topics and sources from my A kids, as the first stage in the paper writing process. It appears from some of them that they aren't taking this thing too seriously, but when they start getting the grades back I think they'll realize that there's really no choice but to do it step by step. Damn it, if I accomplish nothing else with these kids I'm going to show them how to write an adequate paper. Their first effort for Ms. Hill was a disgrace and, since it doesn't appear that the English department does this very well (what the hell are they doing over there?) it's up to me to give them some preparation for college.

Tuesday, November 22, 1994: Lots of prep work for pre-Thanksgiving quizzes tomorrow. I tried to bring it all together—the Indian stuff from the film and lectures, together with all the Western expansion stuff from the book and lectures. I think it worked. In any case I think they now understand some of the dynamics of the time, and why there were two sides to the story (I think I did a little to balance things out for the settlers today). I hope it'll all make sense for tomorrow, because I really don't want to spend any more time on this stuff, as we're falling behind where we should be. In the A class we finished the film and had quite a lot of time to talk about some of the less well-covered aspects of Alexander's Empire. He's such a fascinating character that I'm afraid I'm not doing him justice, but Rome awaits, and time is running out. In any case we had a pretty good class, and managed to cover most of the things, from the reasons he was able to achieve as much as he did, to the reasons his empire fell apart so soon after his death, as well as the legacy he left for the world. That should be enough for the quiz. I'm giving them a take-home quiz on this stuff, an idea I'm not thrilled with, but which seems to be the only alternative, seeing as there's no class tomorrow. It'll be interesting to see if they're responsible enough to bring it in to me at the office, since we're not meeting. I assume that they're concerned enough about their grades to not screw this thing up, but you never know, especially with freshmen. If a bunch of them don't turn it in I don't know what I'll do, though.

Wednesday, November 23, 1994: Thanksgiving is finally here, and can I just say I'm glad November is about over. Maybe an entire month in which there isn't a single complete week of school is great for students, but for teachers, it's hell! You can't get anything going, you can't build up any momentum, and the kids just don't seem to take school very seriously on the day before a day off, therefore giving you even less effective time to work. So good riddance. Even today wasn't complete—my A class was canceled in order to have a pep rally at the end of the day. While I'm all for school spirit and involvement in a community, why did it have to be my A class? In any case, I got the quiz back from **MOST** of them (one exception), so that's one period I'm not going to have to waste on a test, even if I'm a bit wary of take-home quizzes, especially at this level. This should finish the Western expansion stuff, and let me move onto other things. Let me just say that this break couldn't come at a better time—my batteries seem to be running down and I could use a recharge, so I'm really looking forward to the next four days.

Monday, November 28, 1994: Back from Thanksgiving and raring to go. I decided not to go over the quizzes from last week—to let them stand without comment. There were a couple of reasons for this. First of all, we're starting new units in both of these classes, so there's no real point. And second, because we're so far behind that I couldn't afford to waste a day on them. Besides, we spent so much time on these topics that I can't imagine them wanting to do them anymore. So—on to bigger and better things. In the B class we started talking about the way the reform movement grew from its local roots, and some of the directions it took. Then I showed them the film we have on Booker T. Washington, to give them some idea about the direction the Black community was taking in the wake of the failure of reconstruction. The film is quite good, as well as being quite short (thirty minutes), and it gives the perspective, not only of Booker T., but of his main critics as well, especially W.E.B. Du Bois. The film went much better than I planned, they really seemed to be into it, so I think I'll spend tomorrow following up on it. You can't waste an opportunity like this. We talked about the reasons the US started changing from a policy of isolationism to one of imperialism. I tried to stress the physical and social changes that had gone on in the country that led us in this new direction, as I think such forces are far more important than any individual in shaping foreign policy, and I think they at least got the basic idea that when times change, policy often follows right along, but I'm not sure if they understood the details (sometimes I really wish I could get inside their heads and see what's kicking around inside there). In the A class I tried something new altogether. We're going to be starting Rome and, since it stands as a model of success in building and maintaining an empire, I tried to solicit from them some ideas, based on the cultures they've already studied, just what it takes to make a good empire. The answers were surprisingly good in all three areas of domestic, foreign, and colonial, and I was glad to see them thinking in ways they hadn't been before. I'm not sure just how I'll use the list they generated (a better one than I could have), but I'll have to take advantage of such good work at some point. All in all, it was a pretty good day.

Tuesday, November 29, 1994: More good stuff. In the A class I started going into the early history of Rome and its first attempts at expansion. I think I went into too many details about the different tribes involved (they just seem to be important), and I'm afraid we lost sight of the forest for the trees, so I'm going to have to go over some of the larger themes in detail tomorrow. I'm just having so much fun with this stuff—Rome is such a fascinating subject to cover. In the B class we did, together, a worksheet on Booker T. and the film we saw yesterday. I think we went into more detail than they expected, but they seemed to be valiantly trying to keep up, and they really got into it when I began drawing comparisons between the conflict between Booker T. and W.E.B., and the later one between Martin Luther King and Malcolm X (they're more complicated and interesting than they might appear at first). It was a sort of discussion/worksheet combination, but, as long as they wrote the stuff down, I let them hand it in for an easy, good grade.

Wednesday, November 30, 1994: I'm moving away from the book wherever possible, except as a backup for people who weren't in class, so the worksheets are geared towards the content of the lectures/discussions. Maybe they'll do a better job of getting this stuff orally. I sure hope so. In the A class I started by doing what I said I was going to have to do—go over some of the broad themes of Roman history, and then moving on to examples of how, when Rome began to expand the second time, and really began building up the Confederation, it deliberately tried to avoid the mistakes that had resulted in the collapse of its first colonial realm. That's what's so fun about Rome—it makes so much sense that it's almost impossible not to understand what they're doing. However, I am a little distressed at the pace at which we're moving—I had hoped to get through Rome by Christmas, and now this is looking increasingly difficult. But, hell, I don't care—Rome can teach us so much it would be a crime to shortchange it.

Thursday, December 1, 1994: In the A class, I started them on the outlines for their papers. I handed out the stuff I had on what an outline is and how to make one, and then went off on a long, somewhat incoherent, lecture about how to structure a paper, apart from the outline itself. It's funny, I'm such a good paper writer that I thought this would be an easy thing to convey but, as I found out during the class, it's a lot more work than you might expect, and is something that, as a graduate student, you no longer even think about, so it's hard to express. I guess it's like diagramming a sentence—I don't even think I could do it now, but I know how to write one. In the future, I'm going to have to recognize that, for most of these kids, these are entirely new ideas, and give them some examples to work with so as to get a feel for the process. In any case, I think they grasped at least some of the stuff. I guess I'll see when they hand in their first drafts.

Friday, December 2, 1994: Not much to say (yeah, right). In the A class, I continued with the Roman expansion. I managed to get up through the conquest of Italy and the beginnings of the Punic Wars. At this point, I'm just going to have to admit I won't be getting very far into Rome by the end of my tenure. (I can't believe I originally planned to get through the Middle Ages by Christmas!! What a joke!!). I was talking to Dr. Laffey about this stuff and was quite surprised to learn that most teachers don't like teaching World History—they just don't know enough about it to feel comfortable teaching it. I was amazed! I mean, I'm certainly no expert on all of history, but I know a smattering of most periods, and it seems to me that nothing can come close to World History for sheer interest and wonder. And if teachers are afraid of covering it, what does that say about the students who are forced to listen to their timid presentations? Sad, sad, sad.

Monday, December 5, 1994: Man, was I on today. Maybe it was the caffeine from the double cappuccino, but whatever it was—it worked. I was in a teaching ZONE of the type I have seldom experienced before under any circumstances (though all of the ones in the past have been quite memorable). There is no way of conveying in mere words how or why it worked so well, but there was an energy in the room that there has never been before, and I know the kids sensed it too, and responded. What's so amazing about it is that it took place within the context of a rather routine day. The connections between ideas were so clear and easy to articulate that everyone seemed to get them, and I was getting responses out of kids who I've seldom heard from before. I don't know what it was, but if I could bottle it I could make a fortune. In the A class, something even more remarkable happened. I was planning to continue on the Roman expansion, but the kids had so many questions about the outlines for their papers that I ended up spending the entire class going over how to do an outline. I picked a topic with which they all should be familiar by this time, the Peloponnesian War, and outlined it from start to finish, using it as an example of each of the characteristics of a good outline, from the subdivision of topics, to the use of supporting details. All of this was from memory (mine and theirs) and they seemed to have a really good time with it, as did I. Damn, but I wish I knew how to sustain this type of feeling, but I'm only too aware of just how quickly it fades (this must be what the Greeks meant when they spoke of being inspired by a Muse). And it shows just how far enthusiasm can go in the classroom.

Tuesday, December 6, 1994: In the A class, it was a continuation of the Roman expansion, and the conclusion of the Punic Wars (thank God that's finally done). Again, like before, there seems to be a bit of a hero cult developing, as it did around Alcibiades, though this time it's Hannibal who's getting the attention. In my B class, it was the way in which national reform swept across the country with Teddy Roosevelt, and continued on into Taft and Wilson's terms, the causes of WWI, and the alliance system that resulted in the war. All went pretty good, but it raises once again, in my mind, the question of the value of lectures. I've found myself turning to them more and more as the term has progressed, after abandoning them early. Partly this isn't by choice: the last few months have made it abundantly clear that the book we have to work with is not right for these lower divisions. The vocabulary is too difficult, and the writing is too dry. However, there is another reason that strikes closer to the heart, and is one I have addressed before. I'm a pretty good lecturer (this is not time for false modesty). As such, I'm much more willing than other people I know to get up and lecture to a class for fifty minutes or more. But I still don't think lecturing has very much value as a learning tool, and is most likely to be forgotten quickly, regardless of the quality. Nonetheless, as long as I work on the assumption that there's information that they have to have in order to think and write about these historical issues, there has to be some way of getting them this information and, barring the use of the book, lecturing seems to be the fastest way of doing this. However, I'm beginning to question the value of the basic assumption behind this idea—that there's a need to give them this historical information. I think that there must be some way of conveying the ideas of history, without going into detail about the actual events, since these are usually totally irrelevant to the students, at least in the lower divisions. I'm not sure where I'm going with this idea, but it's definitely something to ponder in the weeks and years ahead.

Wednesday, December 7, 1994: <u>Special Note</u>: Tonight was Open House at the school, something I was not looking forward to. I guess I'm still nervous about speaking to parents about their kids, especially being in the position of a student teacher. But it went much better than expected, and I had no real problems. A couple of things worth noting: First, I wasn't really surprised at the turnout, but the numbers were a little excessive, even by the standards I had been told to expect. I saw a total of eleven parental units, ten of which were from the World History and the A level class, and only one from the B. I've both heard and extolled the mantra that parents are the most important factor in the success of a child at school, but this really brought it home. And it was quite frustrating—most of the parents I saw were parents whose kids were doing very well in class, so all I could tell them was "Keep it up," with a few details thrown in. None of the parents I would have most liked to see showed up, and so the whole evening, apart from being a fun exercise in people watching, was curiously empty.

Monday, December 12, 1994: Back from my weekend at James's, a little woozy and worse for wear, but otherwise undamaged. We went over Friday's tests in both the A and B classes, the results of which were generally quite good. I don't know if my own grading curve has slipped, or if the students are getting genuinely better at this stuff, but the grades do seem to be improving. I'm finding more and more that a lot of learning, which should have taken place earlier, goes on when we go over these tests and quizzes. I don't know if it's because ideas previously expressed are being reinforced, or if they are more aware of what they do and do not know, or if it's just that I have a tendency to bring things all together during these discussions but, whatever it is, classes like this always seem to go well. I had planned, in light of the fact that we're doing World War I here, to show the parallels between what happened in Bosnia in 1914, and what is happening today. It started out quite well but, when I started talking about the religious divisions that exist in the country, we got off on a long tangent about what the difference is between Islam, Christianity, and Judaism. At first I was a little reluctant to address such a topic, both because it was not the focus of our discussion, and because it dealt with religious issues that you have to tread lightly on as a teacher, but, when I realized their woeful ignorance of the subject, I decided to jump in to help understand. They were amazed to learn that all three religions have the same source, that they worship the same God, and that Islam, which is quite popular in the class, at least in theory, regards Moses and Jesus as prophets in the same line as Mohammed. We ended up spending much of the class on this topic, and, in the end, I felt quite good about how it had gone, and about the fact that these kids now understand more about these three religions and their relationship to one another than most of the adult population of this country. I think it was a good lesson to learn.

Tuesday, December 13, 1994: This is probably the last day I'm going to get any real work out of these kids, so I tried to get as much done as possible. In my B class, I started to introduce the ideas of interventionism by having a discussion of war, and in what circumstances it might be justified. At first, I was a little surprised at just how isolated most of these kids are, but in light of what's come before, I guess I shouldn't be. But gradually, by bringing up specific situations, like the Nazi advance on the rest of the world, I began to get a little more acknowledgment that perhaps the USA does, at times, have to get involved in the affairs of the rest of the world. A small victory, but at this point I live for such victories, and maybe they'll at least look at the facts next time, and avoid the knee-jerk reaction, so common these days, that the US should get out of other countries and stay at home. I showed a film on some of the new weapons that came into play during WWI, like the machine gun and the submarine, and tried to show how these weapons changed the very idea of war, and depersonalized it to the point that many people thought war had become so horrible that it would never be practiced again (**NEVER** say never). It also was a useful way to introduce the idea of total war, that civilians, as well as combatants, became targets of the war machine, because of the role they played in making war possible. It was an interesting discussion, even if they did seem a little enamored of the new weapons. Finally, in my A class, I concluded the section on Roman expansion and did a quick summary on the decline of the Republic and the Rise of the Empire (boy, did I have to butcher this period). All this was a precursor to the showing of the Roman City film, a truly great piece of educational material (though they didn't respond to it quite as I had hoped). The film reminded me, once again, of just how necessary a remote control is for the showing of educational materials—a pause button would have given me a much better chance to put some of the ideas in context. Oh, well, maybe next time I'll have one, or at least have the gumption to walk up and stop the film every few minutes to make a point.

Wednesday, December 14, 1994: Well, things are beginning to wind down here at Shea. Christmas is only three days away, and there's a distinct spirit of revelry in the air. I'm pretty much winding things down, too, in most cases there's not much more I can do, especially as we have parties planned in all the classes for Friday. So today we basically just goofed off, a trend that's likely to continue on into tomorrow. But even with this attitude, I tried to keep things at least partially focused on history. In my B class, we watched an episode of "Black Adder Goes Forth," a British comedy series that I think is among the funniest ever made. But there was a method to my madness. This particular cycle (there are four, set in various stages of the British Empire) takes place during World War I, the period we're concerned with right now, and it gives a fairly accurate view of what life was like living in the trenches of the war, as well as the problems inherent in leaving them. I was surprised at just how much the kids liked it (I was afraid that they'd have problems with the accents) and further surprised at just how useful it was in bringing up some of the issues of the war, such as the use of propaganda, the shortages soldiers faced, the fear many had of going "over the top," and the differing motivations that guided soldiers into the war. In fact, so many topics were raised that I'm going to have to deal with some of them tomorrow, for lack of time. Overall, it was a highly successful exercise. Finally, in my A class, we watched the second half of the Roman City film, and talked about how it relates to the way Rome ran its Empire, especially how it reflected on the native peoples whom they were trying to govern. Tomorrow, just for fun, I'll be starting Monty Python's "Life of Brian" as a precursor to the rise of Christianity. Personally, I think it's a great film to address this topic, and its portrayal of life in the ancient world is an aspect of the film that's unjustly over-looked. But, as I said before, we're basically winding down, so the main intent of these performances at this point is to have some fun and say good-bye.

Chapter Two

MR. McKNIGHT AND HIS AMAZING COLOSSAL LUNGS! I went back to a classroom, during my spring semester, that I had observed several times before—Mr. McKnight's. I did this for several reasons. First of all, I had been quite taken with McKnight the first time I had met him, so I wanted to see if my opinion had changed now that I had some experience of my own. Second, I wanted to see if Mr. McKnight had found a way to overcome some of the problems I seem to be facing all the time, which might give me a perspective on how I might improve my overall classroom performance. And third, Mr. McKnight and Ms. Hill don't seem to get along very well, and I wanted something to counter the gloom and doom she always seems to be espousing.

I observed McKnight's College US History class, which is similar to one of the classes I'm teaching, so it was interesting to see how he was doing with the same material. He's quite a bit further along than I am, having gotten up to the Spanish-American War, and even I don't expect to cover that for at least two weeks. This might be because he manages to get kids to do homework, at least some of the time. I asked him about this, as Ms. Hill had told me that it was futile to even assign it, and his answer was both encouraging and discouraging. On the one hand, by assigning homework, it freed him up to cover more material in the classroom, something I myself want to do. On the other hand, and this follows a pattern I've been hearing about from all the teachers, getting them to actually do it is becoming harder and harder. Even compared to last year at this time, when I last observed him, he says the students are harder to control, and more poorly prepared, than they had been. Whereas he could count on at least three-quarters of the students to do homework in the past, this year the average is about half. The same goes for grading. He's failing more students this year than he ever has before, half in this class alone, and he doesn't see it getting any better. Even he doesn't seem to know what to do about this trend, though he is less inclined to blame the students than Ms. Hill seems to be (I tend to agree with him on this point, although you can't free students from all the responsibility for their actions). Nonetheless, it does seem possible, with sufficient checks, to get them to do some work outside the classroom.

Another area in which I was keen to observe his behavior had to do with classroom discipline. In this area, Mr. McKnight had his own unique approach—he's so loud that it's impossible for the students not to pay attention or to screw around. I don't know how he manages to maintain his volume for five classes a day, but somehow he does, and the result is a classroom that is filled with energy. When I say volume, I don't mean the bad **"YOU'RE GOING TO BE IN TROUBLE IF YOU DON'T WRITE THIS DOWN"** sort of loudness, but rather the **"THIS IS INTERESTING AND IMPORTANT SO YOU HAVE NO CHOICE BUT TO LISTEN"** sort of feeling. His physical behavior also gives him better control of the classroom—he's constantly walking around the room, through the rows, and even sitting on kids' desks, all the time screaming at the top of his lungs. It is impossible for the students not to listen to what he says.

Another way he maintains discipline is by taking a real interest in what his students look and feel like—he greets each one as they come into the class and is always commenting on how they look or asking how their weekend went. He's also a former football coach (surprise, surprise) and uses this to his advantage as well, by knowing the status of the school teams and which kids in his class are on them. I got the feeling that a lot of the kids genuinely like McKnight, or at least respect him enough to listen, something I have not yet managed in my lower division (though I'm doing quite well with my A class).

Finally, I should say something on how he covered the material. He does a lot of question and answer-type lecturing, and it seems to work fairly well, though I noticed that a couple of the kids were responsible for most of the answers. He does a good job of relating historical events to current ones, using television shows like *Hard Copy* and *A Current Affair* to explain the idea of yellow journalism. He told me after class that if he manages to get the kids to watch these television shows with a more critical eye than they had before, then he had accomplished something better than making them memorize the events of some long-forgotten war. I find it hard to argue with his logic.

Overall, I found my return to Mr. McKnight's classroom to be both beneficial and, to my surprise, frustrating. He has managed to maintain his enthusiasm for teaching and for the students, something I feel I am beginning to lose, and something that Ms. Hill seems to have lost a long time ago. But on the other hand, judging by his results, and by some of the student answers, even he hasn't found a way to reach these students with the material and bring them to the point where they can engage in clear reasoning about complex topics. And, I must point out again: he's failing an awful lot of students, so it's clear even he's having a problem reaching some of the students at all. Despite this, it's good to see a teacher who's still plugging away with the gusto he began with, and I admit there's a lot I could still learn from him. The key will be to find a way to graft his strengths onto my own (though I know I can't maintain his volume; God knows I've tried). Maybe, somewhere in such a synthesis, I might find a middle way that makes me a better teacher and a more useful member of the school community. We'll see.

Chapter Three

JUST WHAT DO YOU TEACH ANYWAY? In a way this type of philosophical diatribe is a good example of what happens when you ask people with an academic background to talk about teaching. While I'm not a teacher yet (at least not in my own eyes), I have had enough experience in teaching to recognize just how useless something like this is most of the time. If you had asked me to write a philosophy of teaching a year ago, I might very well have come up with something lofty about the need to educate in order to keep our country strong, or the need for teachers to give our inner-city students a chance to make it. But those are the words of an academic, looking at teaching from the gilded windows of an ivory tower. Now, as I stand with one foot planted firmly in teaching, and the other still lingering in academia, I find myself in a unique position to respond to this sort of assignment, one that might be seen as less of a philosophy of teaching, and more of a strategy for education.

What struck me most about the students I taught this year is how woefully prepared they were, not just for school, but for life. We sometimes joked that it would be a frightening thing to know that these kids would be electing our future government soon, except it was unlikely that they would ever vote. We said it in jest, but not without a sense of bitter irony—these kids have not been served well by society. By that, I mean far more than just the schools, I mean their families, the social network of our government, the churches and other organizations, and all other groups that these kids have had contact with over the years. None of them have prepared these kids for life, and I fear that, for many of them, they'll spend their entire lives frustrated by their lack of success, and their seemingly endless problems, and never know why. It is with eyes open to this reality that I will be confronting my next teaching assignment, and it is with this thought in mind that I will attempt to help them. Historical facts are so irrelevant to their lives that one is helpless to present them for consideration. These kids need training in basic life skills—pride, responsibility, self-expression, discipline, social interaction. If I can help them develop these things through the use of some history, then good, but it is the skills, not the history, that must be the focus, or else you might as well read them Latin texts, for all the good it's going to do.

Another thing that struck me throughout the semester, and which might point out one way to make the history relevant to their lives, is that these kids are as provincial as medieval peasants. Their whole world ends at the boundaries of their neighborhood and, apart from an occasional phone call to the outside, they have no comprehension of what is going on out there. Forget about what happened in Israel 2000 years ago— these kids have no idea what's happening in Israel today. Hell, forget Israel, they have no idea about what's happening right here in their own communities. They don't know the mayor of their own town, the issues of the last election, or the subjects being debated right now in the state legislature. And their knowledge of national affairs is even more shoddy. How are these kids supposed to make it in the world tomorrow, if they don't know what's going on today? So, as a teacher, I think you have to start with their neighborhood—that is, the community they know—and build outward from there to show them that there is something outside of their world, and it is going to affect them for the rest of their lives, so they'd best know what it is. I'm still not sure how to do this (as I said, I've only got one foot in teaching), but I can't see any other approach having a lasting effect.

Finally, a mention should be made about their skill levels which are, again, woefully inadequately developed. I think that one of the best things a teacher can do, within the contexts stated above, is to concentrate on really developing basic skills in these kids. And I mean **BASIC.** Their penmanship is awful, they can't add, they can't spell, or even put two sentences together to create a coherent thought. I know that most of them are capable of these things, as they generally speak much better than they write, but no one has ever taken the time to sit down with them and help them realize what exactly they have to do. And, again, I think their performance in such areas is closely tied to the things I mentioned above: the lack of self-respect, responsibility, pride, and discipline. It is only by bringing these things all together that any progress can be made.

I've made very little mention of history up to this point. This is quite deliberate. While it breaks my heart, I have to admit that teaching history is not really what these kids need, they need someone to teach them survival. Nothing is more painful for a history lover to admit is that his discipline might be irrelevant to his students, but it's a fact. History might have a place in showing these kids how big the world is, or how to put an idea together, but it fulfills these duties no better or worse than any other subject, from sports, to art, to television movies might. I know how valuable history has been in my own life, in making my decisions, but my background is totally different. One thing every teacher has to realize is that *the kids come first*, and everything else has to remain a very distant second.

Of course, not all kids out there are like my kids this year. They all have different needs; they live in different circumstances. This is why the idea of a teaching philosophy strikes me as so artificial—you have to gear your philosophy to your students. Maybe if I end up at Andover Academy I might find that the student body is better prepared, and that part of the knowledge they require **IS** history, at which point I will be glad to teach the Spanish American War again. Or maybe some kid, some year, will read something about Joan of Arc, and want to know more about her, in which case I will joyfully go back and help them find information about the wars between the French and English. But in every case, my job is as a teacher first, and a history teacher second. And the job of a teacher is to help bring children into adulthood, whatever it takes.

PART FOUR
A Hidden Parallel

As Saren grows older (although he remained a child his entire life) he learns much about the world from his mother, Lithara. But he goes beyond what his mother teaches. He discovers new ways of doing things, things that require more than just an understanding of the natural world. They require an understanding of how to actively alter it to achieve a goal, ways that go well beyond the simple faith in the world and the workings of it that Lithara, or indeed any of the Gods, could provide.

—*The History of Lathrim*

123

Chapter One

One night before my divorce, tears streaming down his cheeks, six-year-old Stephen asked, "Daddy, tell me how long until I die?"

I could find no easy assurance to distract his terror. I tucked him into bed that night and told him a story about God and His concern for all living things and that life after might continue later on in His presence. With an urgent, "Let's talk about God again tomorrow night," he closed his eyes. That began our nightly conversing and brought Stephen's next question.

"Why do we have to die?"

"To make room for more people. Otherwise there would be too many cars and not enough wood to build houses if people lived forever."

"Or there wouldn't be enough food for everybody," he added.

"We're like flowers," I offered.

"God is like steel and bricks and stone." I could see the Deist-in-the-making. "Does God live forever?" he asked.

"Yes."

"Because he has to make more people." Stephen seemed

pleased with this solution.

In the morning, Stephen sang a little song for me as I scrambled eggs and fried bacon for our Saturday breakfast.

"Okay ... k ... k,

Whatever you say ... say ... say.

It's always your way ... way ... way,

Every day ... day ... day."

Stephen ate his crisp bacon thoughtfully, and then he continued his thoughts of the prior evening. "Do you know how sometimes I get happy while I'm sad?" he asked.

"What do you mean?" I reached across the table to brush his sleep-tousled auburn hair back from his forehead.

"Just thinking about God and what He does, about how He makes rain fall, and I think about swimming in the water. And about my birthday and presents."

"What does that have to do with God?"

"Everything! He makes the people who buy the presents." He paused. "If you've been just a little naughty, do you still go to heaven?"

"Not if you're afraid of heights."

"Daddy, that's not funny."

After breakfast, I tried to read the newspaper, but Stephen took me in hand.

"Come on, Daddy. Let's play tackle football."

"All right," I said.

"And we can listen to "Here Comes the Sun.""

It was our favorite Beatles record.

Stephen chased me through the living room and front hallway, shrieking as I circled the dining room table, clutching a small cushion. He caught up to me in the living room and lunged bravely for my legs. He hung on for dear life to my ankle, and we tumbled together to the soft carpet.

"Now you tackle me," he cried, grabbing the cushion.

I let him elude my grasp. Lower to the ground, he took corners with better balance and dashed toward the goal as I tried a headfirst dive, a grandstand play that made him think I'd done my best, skidding on my shoulder across the floor as he touched home triumphantly.

"Did you run your fastest, Daddy?"

He was always testing me, always testing himself. I loved Stephen's courage, welcomed his competition, made him work but let him win. I marveled how strong his drive was to be a man.

"I know why we have to die," he said.

"Why, Hon?"

"God's job is making people. Right? He has to let us die so He can make new people."

"But we have a spirit within us that lives forever," I said. "It's called a soul. It's like the wind."

I blew a gentle breeze in Stephen's face. He crinkled his nose. "That tickles," he said. "Do we start all over again in heaven?"

I hugged him and thought, *I need your love as much as you need mine.*

Chapter Two

"Tell me about when you adopted me," Stephen asked, when he was in high school.

"Do you remember when I called you my beautiful adopted boy?"

"Nope."

"Before I ever told you the story of your adoption, before you could even talk, I'd slip the word into my one-sided diaper-changing talk to you."

"And did I ever ask you what it meant when I could talk?"

"It's very special, I would say. Only a few children can be adopted. We got you from a very special place. You asked me if that's what you were—special? *Yes*, I nodded. And I think you said *I don't want to be one. I don't want to be special.*"

"How did you explain special? What did you say?" Stephen smiled at my difficulty.

"You were playing with your next door neighbor's dog, and I was afraid you were going to ask *Is it like picking out a pet at a pet store?* But you didn't. All I said was that you're my beautiful, adopted boy and I love you."

"Yeah, it meant you were stuck with me," Stephen said. "You couldn't give me back."

"Don't be a wise guy. I remember you told your sister that I said you were my beautiful adopted son, and I got you from an adopted school. Louise couldn't stop laughing. She told you that it wasn't a school, that we got you at a hospital. You said that you could remember things even before you were born, that you knew her already when we got you at the hospital when you were six days old."

"I said that?" Stephen asked.

"You always had clairvoyance, a sort of luminous enlightened way of thinking."

"How old was I?"

"I think you were around five or six when you had this revelation of how you came into our family and what the word 'adopted' meant. About a month later we repeated almost the same conversation. When I asked you *How is my beautiful adopted boy?* you responded *Fine* and asked me again what adopted meant and did it mean I didn't have you? I said, *Yes*, that a young woman and a young man had you as a baby and were not able to care for you and so we got you right after you were born. You were six days old. It was at a special place called the adoption agency. You told me that when you were two years old you remembered I called you that—adopted—and you still thought it was an adopted school you came from.

"And then we started to talk about what is the smallest thing in the world. I suggested a speck of dust. We could see dust motes floating in the sunlight streaming in the window. You said *It's the atom.* When I asked you what the largest was, you asked if it was the pyramids or the Empire State Building. I told you—the universe. You were so happy with that discovery. The next morning you were mad. You said I hate you and wouldn't tell me why. And you kept to your word.

"At dinner table that evening you sat next to me and held my arm. I asked you why you loved me. You said, *Because you're my Daddy.* I asked you why I loved you, and you replied, *Because I'm your beautiful adopted son.* I said, *That's right!* We all were crying by then—your mother and me especially—knowing we were going to get divorced. And then you asked the most wonderful question, *did we adopt God?* I said that sounded like a good idea. You replied *God wasn't born, He was adopted by man. And we adopted God.*"

Chapter Three

I dreamt of Celine whose memory is a ghost I stalk whenever I seek to understand the mystery of life. She had married a second time when I last saw her in New York City 25 years ago. We spent our few days together in cautious harmony, tempting one another with memories of a past so distant, it should have vanished completely. Our lives were never meant to connect, only intersect from time to time. I have known her 50 years in all, yet we have spent less than a month together. I have been influenced by her in unimaginable ways but oddly never dreamt about her until now.

It must have been the discovery of her son's tragic death—crushed under the wheels of a Paris metro—that stimulated my dream. The accident happened the same year my wife and I had taken Stephen to Paris on his spring break from teacher training. At the time Stephen was three years older than her son, strangers to each other, yet touched by a common destiny, touched by the influence that Celine had on all of us. Now, it was a coincidence of grief we shared, to balance our once-up-on-a-time love. How had our separate lives managed to evolve with the same tragic result—the loss of a son?

I dreamt of meeting Celine again and embracing her. She

cradled my face between her hands. I am surprised by her tenderness and ardor, her welcoming me back. We were standing outside her classroom in a Paris lycée, where I had waited patiently for her before. I felt in that moment she had forgiven me for not returning. In the same dream I continued up a steep cliff overlooking the ocean. I am following my own son, who vanished into the ether. I have to fight my urge to leap into the abyss after him.

What can I tell about those strange years that came between us? That I never forgot Celine, that each and every summer in the dusk and heat of some warm day, I would remember our adventure, whose meaning to me grew clearer only as the years went by. She had changed my life, tipped me just a little in the beginning off that safe path I had settled on, a career in a family business. But as the years went by, the tilt away became a wide diverging, like a parallel line gone askew.

• • •

Lycée Voltaire in Paris: I waited for Celine after her class, 20 years after we had first met. She had become both a writer and a teacher. I was divorced by then, as was she. And she, too, had a son.

Four o'clock and classrooms emptied; students rushed for the main entrance. A few remaining boys kicked a soccer ball back and forth in the courtyard. Celine found me outside and took me through the stone corridors on a tour of her school. It was damp and austere as a monastery, a proper atmosphere for learning.

I said to Celine, "You helped me get divorced."

"I know," she replied.

"You said, 'I admire someone who can give everything

he has away.' And so I gave everything away to my wife. I accepted the poverty of my life like a good priest accepts his vows. And I knew it was right to do and that you would have approved. I quit my job, which might have been foolish, or at the least, romantic, but I wanted to change everything—wife, career—to simplify my life in every way, except for my children who, alone, gave me a reason to live. I held them close to me, and that's how I remained sane, kept from jumping out a window like a bankrupt stockbroker."

"Schools have a wonderful way of crystallizing thought, don't they," said Celine. We were standing in her classroom.

We took a subway to visit her friend, Florence, her dearest and best childhood chum. Her apartment was a haven for Celine, where she found the solitude to write. The train rattled and shook. We sat side by side, hurtling through the mass transit tunnel that carried people on their way to work, to rejoin family, perhaps to fall in love. And here, with my oldest love, I felt a sort of hermaphrodite, a transient friend, neither family nor lover, still deeply grateful for what I could share with her.

"Subways remind me of a story by Julio Cortazar. Do you know him?" I nodded yes. "It was about a man who falls in love with a woman on a subway but cannot approach her unless she gets out at a certain stop. That will give him the courage he needs, because it will seem as if it were predestined. He stays on the subway, changing trains to follow her until they are past the stop he has chosen, and, of course, she doesn't get off and when she finally leaves, he doesn't follow her. But every time he rides on a subway, he looks around for that woman again, searching for her, because he imagines her to be his ideal."

"I'm going to follow you when you get off," I said.

"Silly!"

Ile de la Cite: crowds of people on the platform. The train jostled to a halt.

"Come, take my hand. This is our stop."

Near the street an old man, just in front, held open the exit door for us. Once outside Celine leaned toward me in her way that seemed to confide some intimacy. I bent toward her, hanging as I did on her every word.

"In this rude world one of the only signs of friendship, common to all, is holding the door open on exiting from the metro. Even if people are in a hurry, they don't want to let go until you reach it. It's a sort of thread connecting them to you."

• • •

I have a picture of Celine in my office. She gave it to me that time, 25 years ago, when I visited her in Paris. I keep it tucked away in its frame in a corner near my desk and revisit with her when I remember. I did not want to hurt my wife should she come across it at home. Celine is an icon to me, not the love of my life, who, in truth, is my wife. Celine represents a kind of divine spirit, granted in my youth, someone who revered the humble and undefended poor, an idealist in the most platonic sense. The photo, taken by her publisher, shows her with radiant smile, arms outstretched like a holy person welcoming her parishioners—a beautiful woman in her late thirties, with unruly hair, slender in her cotton dress, an aura of light glowing behind her.

Stephen knew this photograph. He also knew of Celine's influence on me. It was difficult to live by her ideals.

"Can I meet her?" Steve asked before our spring break trip to Paris, his last year in graduate school.

In her picture Celine seems to beckon with open arms.

Her face shines with intelligence. She has answers, which I still seek. Why has she influenced me all these years and, through me, my only son? Is it only in Greek myth that we seek our other half to complete the person we might once have been? I look in the mirror and see her reflection staring back. Why did our sons die tragic and violent deaths five years apart? I want to ask her that!

"I don't think I should contact Celine," I told Steve. "It might hurt Sylvia if we did. In all the times we've been to Paris, I never saw her. The last time, in New York, was before I met Sylvia."

For Steve, Paris was a chance to define his own idealism, to explore cathedrals and medieval buildings and indulge his passion for history. We made our decision to go just two weeks before his April vacation and were lucky to get coach seats out of Boston and reservations at the Regina Hotel, where Sylvia and I had stayed on earlier trips.

We each have our own personal Paris. My memories are more a layer cake of love and frustration, of mind opening, and questions never completely answered—first love, first wife, first divorce, then decades of travel with Sylvia, a woman who brought a sense of tranquility into my life. Patient and loyal, generous in her love of Stephen, she allowed us to put our own stamp on this trip during his final year of school. Sylvia even believed for years after, mistakenly, that Steve and I had gone off to visit Celine, never questioning where we had been and, by not, preserving our innocence. She merely accepted it as a life experience for Stephen and me, secure in her own intrinsic beauty, a wisdom I loved in Sylvia, even though Steve and I never made that pilgrimage. In that year of her unknown tragedy, deep in grieving for her son, there is no question, now, that we did the right thing by not intruding.

My memories of Stephen in Paris can be condensed into a narrative of images more painterly than philosophical. Painters, after all, are the mute philosophers who think with their eyes and give us images that tell a whole story—or if the narrative energy fails, simply an impression. And that is what I am left with—Stephen in Paris with his father and stepmother, circa mid 1990s—an impression. I struggle to put his conversations with me into painterly descriptions, into this moving picture set in and around the central elements of Paris—its parks, its museums, the Hotel Regina.

As with all overnight flights to Europe, we arrived at our hotel before our rooms had been vacated and made ready. An old classic, the Hotel Regina faced a small square with a larger-than-life-size bronze statue of Joan of Arc mounted on her horse. It was only nine in the morning. Our rooms would not be ready until after one, so we had a morning to explore Paris nearby.

Around the corner we found a brasserie for breakfast—coffee and rolls, and for Steve, an omelet and a hot chocolate; our first meal together in Paris. And then along rue Saint Honore we strolled, past food shops and boutiques until we came to a quiet street that angled toward the Eglise de la Madeleine, built as a Greek temple, with rows of towering columns and a peristyle with sculptures in the manner of the Parthenon. Just inside, rows of wicker-laced chairs—small and square, hard and upright—reminded us, in the dark interior, they were here for serious prayer.

Emerging into daylight again between Corinthian columns, we could see straight down rue Royale to the Obelisk of the Place de la Concorde. It had come from another

Temple—Luxor in Egypt—three thousand years old. Our history lesson had begun. Beyond the obelisk we could see Les Invalides, the site of Napoleon's tomb.

Few people strolled with us that morning in the Tuileries Garden, the wind at our back down the long stretch from Place de la Concorde, like a fair harbinger to a sailor off on a long voyage. How fatigued we were! Steve's cowboy boots, worn down at the heels, kicked up little sand puffs as he scuffed along the clay path until, at last, we came to the square of Joan of Arc. We passed through the revolving door of the Hotel Regina and went upstairs to our bedrooms.

• • •

As Celine and I walked through the flower market on the way to visit her best friend Florence in the Latin Quarter, I spied bunches of red chrysanthemums. Beautiful flowers, they reminded me of the mums that used to grow every fall behind the house where my children were born. Ruby-rust in color, tall and hardy, they were a lovely harbinger of that rigorous fall season, the return from vacation to school, to work. Our house was perched high on a hill with a marvelous view over woods to the city below, with brown-stained clapboard, red shutters to match the sere autumn colors and the red mums. For a few years I was happy there before I learned about my wife.

"Why did she force you to go to court?" Celine asked.

She shook me from my reverie. "To court?" I asked.

"To keep custody of your son. Why not share him with you? It is always in the child's interest to have his father around. That's why I live so close to Sylvain. Did your wife hate you?"

"I don't think so," I replied. "Really I think it was just an ego trip for her lawyer. He had taken on a cause, defending a homosexual parent. And all I wanted was not to be excluded from my son's life, to still be half the parent I felt he so badly needed."

"What are the circumstances for a homosexual in your community? How would people feel about your wife?"

"She might lose her job."

"That's terrible," Celine replied. "You didn't threaten her, I hope."

"Of course not. The courtroom was even closed to the public."

"Such a difficult life," murmured Celine. "You know; my friend Florence is a lesbian. She lives with a man, but she has affairs with women."

Florence arrived late. We waited patiently for her in the dingy hall of an old building just above rue de la Huchette. Heel sounds clicked along marble stairs, and a tall, elegant woman, legendary childhood friend of Celine, emerged around the corner.

"If I ever had an affair with a woman, it would be Florence," she had said once. "I love Florence because she makes me write better. We have the same opinions." They embraced, and she let us into her apartment. It was like a dark English manor with a huge fireplace and books everywhere. Florence threw her scarf on a couch among silk pillows. As they talked, I went to the balcony to watch the crowd gather in the evening.

"So, you are Joel," Florence turned and said. "I know all about you. I'm amazed you've come back. What took you so long?"

I shrugged. I didn't know the answer.

Celine collapsed on the couch and closed her eyes. "I'm collecting my thoughts," she explained.

"Would you like some tea?" Florence offered.

Each woman had her own writing desk in this room away from their work, their families. I had a cup of tea with Florence, as Celine rested. She asked me if I had read Gertrude Stein and if drugs were a big problem in America.

"Yes," I answered to both, unable to concentrate.

"I tried marijuana," she replied, "and it made me sick. I want to keep my eyes open and my head clear."

I agreed with her. "Coke, dope, booze, mysticism, religion, they're all a way of sinking back into our subconscious animal brain. They all destroy the accomplishments of reason."

"That's very good," Florence said.

I felt happy at her compliment. My life was filling in, becoming fertile. I had kept my promise to return and had met Florence, intimate friend of Celine.

"All right, Joel, you mustn't get too cozy." Celine rose up from the couch well-rested and determined. "We have our work to do now, and you must be dismissed."

"Poor Joel," Florence said. "It was lovely to meet you at long last. I hope you don't wait another twenty years."

• • •

I don't understand why our two sons were fated to die at such a young age, scarcely a few years apart. We are victims of impulse—a fight begun in anger that ends in death, a rush without caution to save another life. Accidents happen in the blink of an eye, before we have time to think, even as the impulse propels us through the portal that separates us from the living.

When exiting a Paris subway, there is not enough space to fall beneath the wheels. Platforms and subway car are engineered with precision, perhaps two inches between the moving car and the stable platform, barely enough room to catch a toe. But I remember now when Stephen and I took the long subway ride to the Basilica of Saint Denis, and as I exited the car, I tripped and someone behind me pushed past and I stumbled toward the rear and saw a small space between the next car behind, just large enough to step off the platform into a dangerous wedge of space. If someone rushing late to catch the open door brushed past a stumbling man and gave him just the push needed to slip one leg off the platform into the void, then he would enter a sinkhole quicker than he could recover his balance. The doors close, the body of connected cars move ahead, inexorable, a powerful machine that pulls him off the platform, dragging his resisting body with grinding force down under the platform and the pitiless wheels.

And so one day Stephen and I traveled to the industrial edge of Paris where, a decade or more later, the urban youth, children of immigrants unintegrated within the life neither of the city nor of France, ran riot through the streets at night, torching automobiles. We left the art deco lobby of the Regina Hotel. At rue Rivoli we waited for the subway train, as three teenage girls nearby watched Stephen and conspired together smiling at him, hoping to get his attention, as if he were some red-haired celebrity they wanted to meet. From Clemenceau we followed the connecting path underground to the Saint Denis line and entered an older subway train with a latch-operated door release that sprang open by compressed air. We stood among the residents of a different Paris—the dark-hued West Africans and the Algerians who lived in the *banlieues* and carried their belongings in black plastic sacks.

"Do you believe in God?" I asked my son.

"No," he replied. "I'm interested in the history of the church and its gothic architecture, not its myths." He shrugged off my questioning as the residual faith of an old agnostic. He knew I was still in the quest for answers.

"I'm sorry I didn't give you more grounding in religion."

"Don't apologize. You did the best you could."

"I didn't want to leave you without understanding the usefulness of prayer."

"It hasn't hurt me that I'm aware of."

"I still pray occasionally," I replied. "Mostly, I just try to stay receptive."

"What do you mean?"

"When that two-hundred-ton airplane is racing down the runway, and I can't fathom how all that weight will get airborne—that's when I pray: 'Please, Lord get this sucker off the ground.' It's never failed me yet."

Stephen smiled. "Prayer didn't have anything to do with it."

"I know, but it makes me feel better."

We cruised along the local subway stops. After Place de Clichy they were all unfamiliar. The train emptied gradually, and we found a place to sit.

"As a child I used to pray every night. I never asked for myself—you know, for things or to win a race, when I was running track. It was only 'Please, Lord, help me to have courage to compete, help me to understand my work. Most important, help my handicapped sister to speak.'"

"She never developed speech, did she, Dad?" Steve asked.

"No. By the time I got to college, I realized it was hopeless. That's when I stopped praying."

"Except on airplanes," he reminded me.

Saint Denis, the first gothic cathedral in France, had sheltered her pilgrims for 10 centuries. As we emerged from the subway into the city square, we looked around, searching for its tall spires. And there, around the Town Hall corner, was the blackened stone portal, one tower strangely decapitated, a massive church encrusted with centuries of air pollution. But inside slender columns supported a canopy of exceptional height, and the church was aglow with natural light.

For me, cathedrals have a way of concentrating spiritual yearning, but Stephen was focused on history, and this church had plenty; itself a great sarcophagus for most French royalty, before their bones were rudely disinterred during the French Revolution. Familiar names—Clovis and Childebert, Dagobert, and Marie Antoinette—had final rest here. Their tombs lay under the altar in crypts and in the chapels and transept of the main church. We stood, each immersed in his own myth—Stephen, the secular, and father, a lapsed agnostic.

"I can prove to you that God exists," I said as we left the church to wander in a nearby park. Above us the Paris sky shone a deep azure blue, the kind of blue we so rarely achieve in a perfectly exposed color photograph.

"C'mon, Dad, don't ruin a good day."

"Why do you say that?" I asked innocently. I knew Steve's take on religion.

"Because you can't prove God exists."

"Well, maybe I can't prove it, but I'll give you something to think about."

"I'm listening." My son had an obstinate tone.

"The Greeks almost had it right," I said. "They believed the Gods could take a human or an animal form. In disguise, Zeus was always abducting some beautiful maiden."

"Dad, those are myths. Don't read too much symbolism into them."

"True, but miracles are all around us. We're alive, right, and we're conscious, and you have to admit most people are curious why that's so. What if we are the Creator's eyes made to marvel at what It has made—a divine image that exists to confirm that It exists through a spiritual longing to be reunited again? We're not the prime mover, but we're smart enough to tinker with creation, discover the atom. We just can't make the leap to believe we are a residual of the Creator."

"Dad, I'm not following you."

"I say the Creator has this need to be recognized, so It creates an extension of Itself, though we're not necessarily made in the same image. The sheer superfluousness of life is like cosmic dandruff sprinkled around the universe. We're proof that a Creator shared Its cosmic consciousness through some miracle of physics and chemistry and math—all those specific numbers that, had they deviated one way or another, would have left a void and no cosmos. And those humans, gifted enough, had the genius to discover theorems and almost understand how it all began. The rest of us just pray."

"For the plane to get off the ground," Steve interrupted.

"So, here we are, walking in this park behind a church named for Saint Denis, a martyr to one of those primitive faiths, who knew, intuitively, more than he could explain that we are just a part of the sound and sight of creation. We're a perfect melody created in spiritual form, a Jesus or Buddha, not as eloquent as they, but divine just the same, incarnate, the spirit of the Creator in all of us."

We drifted farther away from Saint Denis Cathedral into a park with poplar trees. "Steve, what if we could agree that one eternal might exist that connected us to a Creator? Something we shared that made us one and the same."

"There is only the cosmos, Dad, creating itself and destroying itself. It has no connection to us. God doesn't make house calls. God doesn't necessarily love us."

"I'm not talking about human needs, like our hunger for sex that we mistake for love so we can keep the species alive, nor any of the other hungers, thirsts, addictions."

"You mean truth, beauty, and justice?" he asked.

"Something like that… some one important value."

"Dad, truth may be beautiful, but beauty is not truth. It's only a necessary distraction from the ugliness of life."

"How did you become so cynical?"

"It's just true, Dad. Beauty is there to deceive us that someone or something is better or more desirable than some other thing."

"Well, justice is what I mean in a way. An abstract value, not related to survival—something pure and truly eternal."

"Otherwise, it's an indifferent cosmos," Steve replied, "a Deist cosmos. God has no interest in humanity."

We had reached the park's exit. The center of Saint Denis lay several blocks along a narrow street to our right.

"I mean eternal, not an ideal. I think Plato set us in the wrong direction, trying to be an arbiter of beauty and form. My father used to say an ugly mutt was a healthier animal than the dog with a pedigree. He was just a farm boy who knew that inbreeding was bad and a wide gene selection made an animal stronger."

"We're getting off subject, Dad."

"All right, not human truths, not ideals—an eternal! Something that exists in all sentient beings. Like affection, not sex; nurture in its selfless, parental, protective way; fairness, which I think is a very advanced eternal."

"Nothing is fair, Dad."

"I differ with you, Steve. I think people have an innate sense of what is right and wrong, not what is true, but what is fair. People instinctively do what is fair."

"That's a commandment—do unto others as you would have others do unto you."

"It's why we make compromises, and it's what leads us to the abstract idea of justice, just as affection leads to an abstract of love, not to sex, but to a pure, nurturing love, caring selflessly for someone who needs our care. I think the needy bring out our sense of nurture. That's why I've always mistrusted leaders who have never reared children. They've never had their nurture gene stimulated."

"So, what is the one eternal you think can prove the existence of God?" Steve asked, still unconvinced.

"Curiosity," I said.

"Curiosity?" he exclaimed. "That's not an eternal."

"Oh, yes!" I smiled. "We're always asking questions. Infants look at you, just bursting with curiosity. They can't learn speech fast enough to ask those questions children ask—what's this, what's that? What are we going to do next? And as adults we want to know *why* are we here in a cosmic void on this planet full of miracles, full of life in every crevice and patch of space, in the depths of the darkest sea? All life is questing, curious to explore its surroundings, sensitive to heat, to light, to cold, absorbing, ingesting whatever nutrient is nearby, and multiplying in a way that helps it survive until it falters, dies, mutates, or evolves into something better able to survive. Life casts its seed on the wind, in murky plumes in the sea, primitive animal or plant or fish; and the rest of us mammals explore the curious opposite sex in order to connect at the fertile place we so burn with curiosity and desire to intersect at."

"You mean fuck, Dad. Go ahead, say it… fuck! We're back to sex now."

"That's just one part of it," I replied. "We survive by being curious. Curiosity leads the way to learning, to survival. It is its own reward. Dolphins are curious about us. We teach them tricks and think of them as friendly, so we pass laws not to catch them with tuna in the same net, because we only like to eat tuna, not dolphins. But dolphins are not our friends; they're just curious, like us."

"Sometimes we die with curiosity," said Steve. "Curiosity killed the cat."

"Humans are the most curious of all. We have large brains and a consciousness of who we are. And consciousness is the greatest miracle. Trees may be sensitive to light and their surroundings, but they can't think. Even so, they do something that makes them our first cousin."

"I know… I know. They breathe in our carbon dioxide and breathe out oxygen."

"We're in the temple right here, *outside* this cathedral in Saint Denis square, on this marvel of an Earth where miracles are happening all the time. We're just too obtuse to see them."

Stephen smiled. "So, we have consciousness and we stand upright and we have very sensitive eyes. I remember you were always making me look skyward, and you bought me a telescope. For a while I even wanted to be an astronomer, and, after you took me to an Isaac Asimov lecture, I read all the science fiction I could find about space travel. Okay, we're curious, and curiosity leads to experimenting and to discovery.

And all sentient life shares curiosity, so what does that have to do with a Creator?"

"God is more curious than we are. That's why It created us on this vulnerable but hospitable Earth, in this fragile flesh and form, so that It could see Itself. We are a wisp of the Creator made sentient in order to be perceived by Its own reflection. We, who yearn to know why we are here, are just a reflection of the Creator, wanting to be recognized, eyeballing one another in a cosmic mirror, because eyesight is the ultimate reflector. The Creator sees us trying to see the Creator. We are so curious to understand, and every one of us, in some fashion, feels this spiritual yearning.

"That means we are incarnate," Steve said. "We're all divine, not just a few sensitive souls like Jesus and Buddha and Mohammed."

"That's my theology."

"And for what purpose?"

"We discover ourselves, our true nature. We try to live reverent lives and be fair. Fairness brings justice, as nurturing brings love. Descartes said: *'Cogito ergo sum. I think, therefore I am.'* He knew consciousness was the key. But I say: We think, therefore we are divine."

"I might buy that," Steve replied. "Let me think about it."

• • •

"Come, I'll introduce you to my son," said Celine. "He's taking his bath."

Her small apartment was comfortable and very appealing, with bare wood floors and a few worn Oriental rugs, lamps to read by, and cozy chairs to sit in. Bookcases. At one end of the living room, a door gave entry into a long bathroom. In the

148

bathtub, up to his armpits in warm, soapy water, surrounded by his toys, sat Victor, five years old.

"Victor, this is Joel. Say '*bonjour*.'" Little Victor stood up and looked at me with little interest. "*Bonjour*," he chirped like a sparrow, then sat down and resumed his naval games. She knelt at tub side, took a washcloth, and began to scrub her son's back. He was a beautiful boy, and Celine attended him with unusual deference.

"Pour coffee yourself," she said. "I've already eaten. There is bread and jam if you like."

The bread was stale but tasty with fresh butter and plum preserve. I stuck in my knife and pulled out a plum and thought "What a good boy am I." A dressed and dried Victor examined me with cautious disdain and went about his morning play. We were going shopping and then to have lunch with Celine's friend and her son, who was the same age as Victor.

In a loose-fitting blouse and a baggy skirt, Celine emerged once more, still toweling her damp hair. "Here is the key to Pierre's flat. It's across the street, number eighteen, about two buildings down. Go to the concierge and tell her you'll be staying there for a few days. Leave your bags, and I'll be ready by the time you return. All right, *cheri*?" She smiled.

Pierre was going to move in with Celine temporarily, although I didn't understand why they weren't living together now. It was a typical young man's apartment, sparsely furnished and dirty in those places one lacked patience to keep clean, like the bathroom and the kitchen. There were two dirty coffee cups in the sink and an empty bottle of Courvoisier on the counter. But the bed had crisp, clean sheets and a down-filled quilt and was much more comfortable than my hotel bed. I put my bags away and rejoined Celine.

"Will you buy me a gift?" Celine asked as we rode in the cab. She sat in the rear seat with Victor, while I sat up front.

"Whatever you like," I replied.

"Not an expensive one. I do need two combs. You know like this, to hold my hair back." She held it away from her face over one ear, her marvelous hair full and curly like a Gypsy woman. She directed the driver to a fashionable area for shopping.

I turned around and looked out the front window. We passed the Sorbonne, and I recognized rue des Ecole. I felt Celine touch the back of my hair lightly. It was an unexpected caress, like a shared reminder of 20 years before on that same street.

We stopped at a store in Place Saint Sulpice. Celine picked up some linen her friend Catherine had ordered. We visited several more shops. I bought Victor a puzzle toy that had to be assembled. Celine chose two combs and realized she needed a mirror for her purse. We found some metal discs painted like jar caps on one side, polished on the other. They were inexpensive and ideal mirrors. "Buy several," Celine urged, "and keep one for yourself. *Look in the mirror, and you will always remember me.*"

At Catherine's apartment the two children ran off to amuse themselves. They were precocious friends who often played together. The apartment had a penthouse roof and a lovely view. We could hear the children arguing. "Like a good communist and capitalist," said Catherine. There were books scattered all around the apartment. Catherine's ex-husband was a successful newspaper publisher.

Catherine was another of Celine's childhood chums. They were involved with a small press that published commentary on communism outside Russia. I felt excluded from their conversation and wandered off to play with the children, while they prepared lunch. I helped Victor assemble the puzzle game, and as I knelt on the floor, I was suddenly assaulted by the two of them. They jumped on me, laughing, while I pretended to be Gulliver tormented by Lilliputians, until the call to lunch rescued me.

We sat in comfortable chairs on the roof patio and ate goat cheese. We drank pastis and water. Catherine served cold roast chicken, sliced sausage, raw cauliflower, and tomatoes. A warm September sun shone, and as the clouds thinned, we sat back to enjoy it.

"Take off your sweater," Celine insisted.

I stood up and pulled my sweater over my head. Behind me I heard Celine shriek.

"Oh my God. I remember everything."

"What is it?" Catherine asked.

"It's Joel's underwear with the red elastic band. I remembered Segovia. You wore the same underwear with a red band. It brought the memory back so strong."

"He doesn't change his underwear," Catherine joked.

"Can you imagine?" Celine said. "Twenty years, and I still remembered. You still have a wonderful body."

The two young boys went inside to resume their games.

"It's so restful when they leave," said Catherine.

"When does a male child become less dependent on his mother?" Celine asked.

"At forty," I replied.

"Thirty-five more years!" she exclaimed. "My God, I won't last that long."

"Really at about age eight." I smiled at her relief.

"Why didn't you return to Paris sooner?" Catherine asked.

"I met a young woman and married her a year later."

"Just as I had predicted for him," said Celine. "A nice New York girl, very materialistic."

"Is that true?" asked Catherine.

"Making a lot of money was never that important to me. That worried my wife. She was a very practical woman."

"Who is your favorite American writer?" Celine asked.

"Saul Bellow," I replied.

"Mine too," she said, quite surprised. "Have you read *Herzog?*" I nodded yes. "A marvelous book. No one in France can write like that."

"I once shook Saul Bellow's hand." They looked at me with amazement.

"It's true. At my fifteenth college reunion. Bellow was awarded an honorary degree. I was a class marshal at commencement and walked around in a top hat and tails. Masquerading as a success in that costume, I approached Bellow, who was standing by himself after the ceremony near the library. I extended my hand and told him the usual stuff about admiring his work. He gave me a fishy look and a weak handshake. Brought me nothing but bad luck. Like some helpless Bellow character, I discovered soon after that my wife had a woman for a lover. It was all downhill from there." Celine and Catherine both laughed.

Suddenly, we heard the children screaming. The two philosopher/mothers sprang out of their chairs and rushed inside to see what had happened.

"Julian pissed on me," screamed poor Victor.

"He pissed on me too," sobbed Julian.

"But Julian pissed first," said Victor.

And we all laughed.

• • •

We had a quiet ride back to the center of Paris. The cars were empty at first, and we picked our seats together. Late in the afternoon they filled with people returning home, somber folk, fatigued with their day's effort. Rubber tires of the subway car hummed beneath us, the brutal weapon that had crushed Celine's son, as Stephen would be mercilessly wave-battered against rocks before he drowned in a strange ocean far away.

And thus the crux of my dilemma, the question of all who suffer loss—from Job and Joseph the carpenter to a parent in wartime—why were Celine and I chosen to suffer the death of our only sons? Were we punished by some cruel tormenter for discrete sins against ourselves, for fetal lives taken, or some other misdeed we could not possibly fathom? Not destined to live our lives together, we had come together three times and parted each time. How could we reconcile our loss unless its purpose was still unfolding?

• • •

The young girl I had met in Spain became a mother who regretted she did not kiss her son good-bye that fateful day when he left home. History obsessed me—the ephemeral young Celine of 50 years past—she at age 16, and I, 21, exploring the Church of Vera Cruz. We had met by accident at the hotel.

"Have you seen any of Segovia yet?" she asked.

"Not much," I said.

"Come," she insisted. "While there is still light, I'll show you a place I love very much. It's the Church of Vera Cruz."

Segovia was small enough to traverse in minutes. Below

the wall that encircled the town, we crossed a stone bridge and climbed a hill on the opposite side of Segovia from the mountains. At the edge of a steep embankment stood the small Church of Vera Cruz, its 12 sides curved symmetrically around the short tower that rose from one end. We stopped a moment, charmed by its beauty, and then hurried from the road across a field to the entrance.

Inside Vera Cruz the walls rose over us, blending into a cupola. In the center a hollow column extended from the floor to the ceiling. Stairs led inside to a raised level, a tiny space within the greater chapel. We climbed up and, through an opening, could see the main altar with its wooden figure of Christ stretched austerely above.

"Before going off to Holy Wars, the Knights Templar would come here to pray," Celine explained.

We continued across the field, with Celine leading a few steps ahead until we reached the hilltop. The sun disappeared to our right in a red glow, and on either side gently rolling plains extended. Perched on the hill directly in front was Segovia: the cathedral rising above the rooftops, the castle, with its tall spires, at the city's prow. It was a cluster of small buildings glowing in the day's last light.

"It's beautiful," Celine said. "Someday I'll write about this evening."

She seemed young and wise at the same time. My hand touched hers but I hesitated, afraid to betray our strange harmony.

An evening chill began to settle. "Shouldn't we go back?" I asked. "Let me help you down this embankment." I climbed carefully down the rock, and stood, waiting for Celine.

"Let's do a cinemascope—like in the movies," she cried.

"Catch me!" Then she jumped the few feet that separated us, and I helped her balance when she landed. It was the first time we touched. We started to walk through a plowed field. She stopped suddenly and said, "We shouldn't do this. The farmer may have planted potatoes here, and we might destroy them. You know, they are so poor in Spain. It's a calamity if even a single potato is destroyed." We circled the field instead, and passed the Chapel once more.

"I love your right arm," she said impulsively. "Will you give it to me as a gift?"

"Of course," I stammered.

"Where will you go from Segovia?" Celine asked.

"I don't know… maybe Portugal."

"I wish you wouldn't leave," Celine said. "Oh, if you could only have something happen so you would have to stay here. Stay… Please stay."

"A few days," I promised.

"I want to smell you, so I can remember tonight." And impulsively, she pressed her face against my shirt. I put my arm lightly around her shoulder.

Later, in a dark street, we stopped again. Were we alone? Celine let go of my arm, and we stood, facing one another. The street sloped gently down. I stood in front of her, and our heads were almost even. "I want to kiss you," she said softly. With a sweetness I shall always remember, she pressed her lips gently to mine. I let my hands rest softly on her back, and when she moved closer, we clung together tightly, like two lovers who had long been parted.

"Tomorrow," said Celine, "we shall go for a ride far in the country and we can lie in the fields and I can kiss your face."

And so I have been truant in Celine's life, never returning

to stay, yet always curious about her. When we met in New York, she was a sophisticated 40-year-old woman—attractive and confident, quite stylish. She was like a goddess descended to Earth in human form, incarnate, my avatar.

"Did I tell you I married Pierre?" she said. I had met him in Paris four years earlier.

"No," I said, somewhat shaken.

"Last fall. He insisted. I didn't want to. He is younger than me, as my father is younger than my mother. I fell in love with Pierre when I separated from Sylvain. Just before you came back to Paris. When Victor was born I thought he might be Pierre's child. I had such tremendous guilt. I'm very fertile. Just last year I had an abortion. Pierre wants me to have another child. But I'm not sure. I have too much to do. What do you think?"

"I don't think it's a good idea," I replied, happy that she had asked my opinion.

"Why?"

"You know how much energy it takes to care for a child."

"I'm worried about my age. Anyway, my son Victor would not be very happy either."

• • •

Stephen died on a lovely Sunday afternoon. His stepmother and I had returned home from a concert—Bach's *Goldberg Variations*—played with inspiring grace by a young harpsichordist. It's odd how we think of lovely weather as God's benevolence shining on our lives. If the weather is fair for a wedding day, we like to believe God is favoring us with added good luck. Or at a funeral we feel the person who is lowered into the ground has a far better chance of going to heaven if the sun is shining than if it's pouring rain—benign superstition that does no harm.

On that same day, the weather had cleared in Nicaragua, where Stephen lived and taught history at The American School. A hurricane had just passed across the narrow ismuth of Nicaragua. Stephen and his friends had planned a trip along the west coast on a Pacific schooner, canceled because of rough seas that still lingered after the powerful storm. Nevertheless, they had stayed there on the coast, watching the ocean uncoil each long wave into a force crashing against the rocky coast, until his friend's dog slipped off the rocks into turbulent surf, and Stephen leapt in to save him.

I am reminded of an ancient Sumerian paradox concerning the eternal and its numinous force, which resides in everything. "You, who are not the cream, were poured out with the cream. You, who are not the milk, were drunk with the milk."

So it is with Celine and so it is with Stephen. You, who are not my life, have always been my life.

PART FIVE
Shoreham

Saren receives a request from Bashad to teach his children literacy. Bashad, seeing the lawful effects of language elsewhere in the world, hopes that written language will have a similar effect on his children, bringing them into the lawful fold. Saren agrees and travels to Kharga. There, much to his bafflement, Saren is met mostly by indifference (although he does become the butt of a lot of practical jokes). When he shows patience and a good sense of humor, some stay with him long enough to learn numbers (to keep score of games) and written language (so that the 'best' jokes would be remembered forever). But few care enough to learn. Baffled by his failure, Saren studies the Baradelim Range before striking east across the Sea of Grass.

—*The History of Lathrim*

Chapter One

In 1995, his first year out of graduate school, Stephen signed onto the substitute teacher's list with the City of Providence. One had to climb the ladder of seniority to get a full-time job, do the penance of babysitting classes all over the city in all subjects. With discipline problems in this predominantly inner-city system, it was daily student target practice and new teachers fair game. Within a month Steve substituted for a teacher who got hurt breaking up a fight between two boys in his English class, at Central High School, the largest multi-ethnic, inner-city school. It wasn't Steve's subject but once called as a substitute, he was allowed to keep the class as long as the teacher remained out of work.

I can remember Steve's excitement, dreading the teacher might return and claim his classes back. His challenge—to create a curriculum in a subject for which he hadn't been prepared and surmount the problem of English as a second language among many of his Asian, Hispanic, and Liberian immigrant students. He went rummaging through the archives of old textbooks stored in the cellars of Central High School and came up with a ninth-grade text to replace the fifth-grade text the injured teacher had been using. Steve flunked most of his students that first marking period and challenged them to do better. He worked with them on individual writing assignments, correcting their grammar and context, urging them to trust their spoken word as a basis for expressing their ideas. He'd help them shape language into clear expression. Later in the year he took his brightest volunteers and organized a team to compete in mock trials against other senior high schools. And they actually won some of their competitions.

The school administration left Steve alone to follow his own goals. There were hazards enough in the school. Someone stole his wallet. His portable CD disc players disappeared one after another. His car was stolen. But given the chance, Steve made a difference in his students' lives. Most of them passed his course. They read more challenging work and they learned how to write about it. These were basic skills needed to survive in life and teaching them to his students gave him a new determination not to waste his own talent.

But the system decreed that a certified English instructor replace him the following year. Back into the substitute pool he plunged, hating every assignment to nursemaid unruly kids, a day at a time, never longer than a week—in all subjects from cooking to woodworking. Seldom history, the subject he adored. Two frustrating years followed and all during that time he perfected his resume and sent it out to other communities and other states, attending job fairs in distant cities, seeking interviews for a full-time teaching position in history.

After several interviews he was hired to teach middle school on Long Island, New York. He accepted with trepidation, not completely confident he could control his classes, teaching the difficult early teens. He'd always had trouble in the middle school. But that was substitute teaching. This time they'd have to face him every day. He could deal with it, if the school gave him support.

The pay scale was phenomenal by local standards. He would finally have his own classes. He took the job and deeply regretted it.

In just a month and a half, by mid-October, the school took his classes away from him—just after the first marking period. Bad judgment or unreasonable accusations? He thought he was handling the academic side okay. Perhaps he had graded them too hard. No doubt many would earn their A grade by semester end. Maybe the work was too hard for them. He challenged them to think as he might a senior high class. Were they ready to be drawn into controversy, since that's what most of the complaints were about—the pejorative word for Black used in context when studying original documents from the Civil War, the film *Glory* shown in class, about a courageous Black infantry division that won Denzel Washington an Oscar. A book assignment that parents complained had the word "bastard" in it; the book banned.

"God," his favorite expression of frustration, "I thought this was a liberal community!"

School protocol made it necessary to be friends with your students, take them out for lunch, exchange e-mail, and share their lives. One girl wrote him love letters which he tried to discourage. Someone asked if he were gay, because he walked "funny," that odd pigeon-toed shuffle in his heel-worn cowboy boots. What next? One of his students vowed to get him fired. "I just don't understand why this kid hates me."

One calamity followed another, until someone discovered his AOL profile, written when he connected to the Internet in graduate school. It was a bit of history borrowed from Chuck

Colson, aide to President Nixon: "If you've got them by the balls, their minds and hearts will follow," his own ironic take on a teacher's role. Taken out of context the quote led to a speedy dismissal, without trial. Stephen was out of a job, saddled with an expensive apartment lease.

Chapter Two

Teaching Journal, 1997–1998:

All right— what I'm looking to do is create a new teaching journal to serve as a basis of comparison to the one I wrote while at Shea for my teaching course. Ultimately, I want to go back and compare the two, without compromising my new experiences as NEW. I will not look at the old journal during this process. Only at the end of the year will I go back and revisit both experiences to see what I might have learned from them.

This is day one at the new school. I'm still not sure that I've gotten the job, as the question of certification still needs to be answered, but I'm hoping that will be resolved shortly, especially since I'm currently commuting here from James's in Huntington, and while the commute isn't too bad (forty-five to fifty minutes each way), it is taking up time I might better use in other ways. I'm very nervous about this whole thing— besides teaching a different grade, and an entirely different type of student, in middle school, this whole place seems a little touchy-feely to me. I have no idea what to do about this advisor thing, I'm hoping the students can help me find my way through it, and the idea of them eating lunch with me every day is certainly a little odd. I've never seen a school without a cafeteria before. Plus, I have the added burden of replacing a man who would seem to have been the most popular teacher in school history, so there are some pretty big shoes to fill. It's now 10:30 and we just got back from the big meeting at the high school to welcome everyone back—as well as everyone new. Mr. Cary, the principal, seems to be popular with everyone here. I did detect more than a little tension between the administration and the unions, which I suppose should be expected, but it was not fun to behold on the first day.

I've been working to get my room in order for most of the day. I got rid of most of Mr. Burkhart's slide stuff, as well as anything that might make the room interesting. It's now as generic as a McDonald's. One of the things I hope to do with the students is to make this place ours. We can work together to decorate it and make it more distinct. We'll see how that goes—I might mention it to the kids tomorrow. Speaking of tomorrow, I'm still not sure exactly what I'm going to be doing. I want to get to know the kids, so I might spend time just interacting with them. I'm not sure about the long double-period class though. I just got the good news, however, about books. I can order any books I like. Now I'm getting excited! Everyone's been very nice and helpful so far, though we'll see how far their sincerity goes when faced with a real problem. In any case, I'll know by tomorrow if I'm really going to be staying here.

Officially it's the first day of school. The students showed up this morning. First impression: pretty good. Everyone was here (that's certainly new), they were relatively quiet, and the one kid who was a smart-ass was easy to handle, at least so far. I might have to work to bring them out a little, but hey—it's the first day and I'm a new teacher. We'll see how they are in a month.

It didn't take long to discover in my double-time class—you need to have things for them to do. The first half was OK, though more disorganized than I would have liked (my fault). During the second half we had a fire drill that kept the kids outside for twenty minutes, which saved me from being poorly prepared. But the feedback I've gotten from the kids already is positive, though the quiet ones seemed to be bored and slightly annoyed by the attention the loud ones got. I've got to start working on learning names—that's going to be tough, but I want to do it immediately. The class seems controllable; they quiet down when I tell them to, but I'm going to have to be more assertive to set the tone. I'll try that in my later classes.

By the end of the day, I had my other three classes. They seemed to go OK too, the same strengths and weaknesses as before. We did the "Why do we study History?" bit in all three classes, with mixed results. Just shows once again that lecturing is not the best way to work with kids, something that I've got to keep telling myself, lest I fall into the lecturing trap. I'm not sure what I'm going to do tomorrow yet. I need a lesson that will get them involved. And I'm going to have to be more aggressive in calling on people, both for the names and for the involvement. In any case, I did seem to achieve one of my goals today—the kids seem to like me, a foundation on which a class can be (carefully) built.

I have an assignment for them to do today that will be due Monday (give them the weekend if they want it). It's on the future, and what they think the future will be like, especially in relation to them. They are to write about their job, family, housing, transportation, country, and the biggest changes they see happening over the next twenty years. I'm hoping this will give me both an idea about how well they write, as well as gaining for me some personal information about how these kids see themselves. The initial reaction this morning in advisory was, shall we say, not positive, at least to the idea of a writing assignment so early in the year, but we'll see what they think once they see what the assignment is. In any case, I'm experimenting with the idea of having high expectations of my students, something that has been a luxury until now, in the hope that they will learn to have such expectations for themselves, and discover that they can live up to them, regardless of how difficult they might think they are.

I just had the double class and it went great, really great. These kids were able to focus for most of eighty minutes on what the world of the future might be like. Most of them really seemed to get into it, and their imaginations were running wild, maybe a little too wild in some cases. There were a few who seemed vaguely troubled by the assignment, at least they didn't seem that enthused. Many of these were the same kids who were so quiet yesterday. I'm going to have to pay more attention to the quiet kids this year—they might very well have something great to say, and just lack the confidence or conviction to bring it out. I'll have to be careful how I handle it, and it might not work, but I want to do what I can to bring everyone along on this journey, loud and quiet alike. I only have one year to change their lives—I have to take advantage of every opportunity.

The lessons went well in my other classes, although best in the ¾-period class. I'm getting a good feeling about that group, though I think I'll have to sit on them to keep them focused. It's amazing how strong a correlation there is between the troublemakers in a class and the ones who sit in the back. I'm not surprised by this, it's only natural, but it's still quite amusing. And it crosses both sexes. Tomorrow we're doing current events, so we'll see just what they know about the world and nation. I'm not expecting much, but I'm hopeful. Overall, I'm still getting a good feeling about these classes, though we'll have to see when I do a lecture. I need to learn the names of everyone, especially the troublemakers, if for no other reason than so I can call on them at inopportune moments. Ahh, the devious ways of the teacher.

I HATE MY CAR! I know that isn't related to teaching, but since it might color the rest of my day, I thought I should mention it. I'm having sporadic problems starting it. I'll get it fixed this weekend, but I have to get there for that to happen, so I'm keeping my fingers crossed.

We studied the Middle East and yesterday's bombing in Jerusalem. It ended up being, (shades of student teaching) basically a lecture about the history of Israel and its clashes with the Arabs. The kids did know a lot about what's going on, but I think I went into too much detail, going through the various wars and peace accords. However, I do think the content was good and the kids did learn something about the Middle East, and what's going on there. I'm going to try, in the rest of the classes, to focus on more of the general questions of current events, and less on the specifics. I also want to get the kids more involved with the process. I'm still going to start the same way, reading an article from *The New York Times* as if on the scene as it happens and try to get them to see both sides of an issue. I got a volunteer to be newscaster next week (big surprise) so maybe it'll work out better when I'm giving up some control to the students. There was a meeting of all 8th grade teachers this morning, something that's supposed to happen once or twice a week. Pretty dull—with a lot of bitching and moaning about the new policies on homework and other general things. I can see that these teachers care about the students, but there's also a lot of ego involved, and a lot of territoriality. I'm going to try to stay quiet at these first few meetings, maybe even for the month, just so I can get a sense of the personalities and group dynamics of my peers. As the saying goes—You have two ears and only one mouth for a reason.

Well, I must admit, I'm feeling a little drained. It has been exhausting moving into a new apartment, and fighting the battle to keep the ¾ class on task and under control. The one bright spot is that I started reading the stories the kids wrote about the future. By and large, they are great, I mean truly great. Much better than anything I have seen, both in writing quality and in their confidence in themselves and in their imagination. I'm impressed.

I was glad when today ended. As I desperately flail about looking for things for the double-period class to do, and with all these papers to grade, I came up with an idea. I hope this isn't copping out, but I'm planning to show the kids the movie, *Glory*, over the next few days. It's not directly related to the topic at hand, the Civil War and Reconstruction, but it's a great movie, and it does give a good sense of attitudes both towards and among Blacks during this period, as well as what fighting in the Civil War was like. Now I just have to see if I can get it approved. Maybe I'll just show it, and see what happens. If I get in trouble I can just plead ignorance, and there are few movies that might offend some that are easier to defend than something like *Glory* (except maybe *Schindler's List*). In any case, I'm beginning to see different personalities emerging in these classes. Third period is generally good, except for a few, like Ryan and Mark, who make it very difficult. I'm going to try sitting on them hard from the beginning and see what happens. Seventh period is the quiet class of well-behaved students (it's also small, no wonder). Eighth is the BIG class, and there are TWO problems—the girls in the back of the room, and the boys in the back of the room. This class is never really quiet, and I'm not sure what's going to work to bring things down to a manageable level here. Ninth is like third, a few problems and the rest generally good. Ninth has the most personality of all the classes, but it also has the most difficult discipline problems. I think I'll try to focus in on one or two of them and see if the rest fall in line. In any case, with the movie, I'll be getting a little breathing room on these assignments, and hopefully that will be enough to get me through next week, after which things should run a lot more smoothly. I've also begun to schedule meetings with my advisees, starting tomorrow with Adam. That is auspicious! I had a meeting with the school psychologist this morning about my advisees. He gave me a bit of useful information that should help me get to know these kids better, and to understand them.

The movie has gone over well, so far. I made the mistake of letting some of the kids see the box it came in, and they immediately keyed onto the fact that it's rated R. I think it's mostly for the violence, but there is a bit of profanity as well (I still cringe every time I hear the word "fuck" in the film [it is only once so far, but I've now heard it 4 times]). We'll see if there's any fallout. I do have a backup film ready—parts of Ken Burns' Civil War series. In any case the kids seem to be enjoying the film, and there were no real problems today. My biggest concern now is with the papers. They're taking an incredibly long time to grade. I spent most of the day working on them and I've gotten through less than one class. I might have to cut corners when it comes to the rest, or I'll never be able to give a written assignment again (or it will never be done). But there have been some good ones, and none that I would characterize as truly BAD. I think that in the English class I will have to do some focused grammar lessons, such as the difference between 'there,' 'their,' and 'they're,' and especially one on commas, since these do seem to be areas in which everyone is having a problem. I'm also starting the long (and becoming familiar) struggle to fairly grade the papers as well. I forgot how much of a problem this is, and it's become especially acute now that I'm in a school in which grades actually matter. I foresee problems in the future with this. I can certainly see what makes standardized tests so attractive to teachers in schools like this. It's a way to cover your butt, a way of coming up with grades that the kids can't argue with (or the parents). I got back most of the homework assignments, and most of those were even done correctly, though there are those who are going to have to learn that following directions is an important part of success. Hopefully, a few bad grades based on directions will wake them up.

The other shoe dropped regarding the film. Mr. Cary called me into his office to tell me that there had apparently been some complaints (or at least that some were coming) and that there was a problem with showing an R-rated movie to these kids (big surprise). Apparently there was a problem with this last year (with "Schindler's List," of all films) and there is now a procedure for getting parents' permission to see a film that is not G or PG rated. Well, I knew it could happen, and Cary was quite nice about the whole thing, especially when I explained that I had given the kids the option of not watching the film (I think that helped save my ass, especially if parents actually complain that I made their kids watch the film). But I do get to finish the film, so I guess it's not too bad. Also, in what might be big news, Peter, the other teacher who's teaching a split schedule (4 English / 1 Social Studies), apparently has been making a bit of a fuss, and so Cary asked me about the possibility of switching things so that I have five social studies, and he has five English. YEA!!!! I'll get rid of that damn class for half the time, though I'm not sure about the new bunch I'll be getting. Oh, and I began to get some complaints from the kids about the amount of work. I gave them an assignment based on the film about the motivations of the main characters, and about what they might be willing to fight and possibly die for. It's not due until next Friday, so they have plenty of time (500 words—no big whoop). I also gave them some first-person accounts of slavery and its immediate aftermath, asking them to compare and contrast these experiences.

Well, the idea fell through, so I'm stuck with my home room class for the year. Oh, well. Well, tonight is the first PTA meeting, so I'll be able to see if this movie thing is going to get out of hand. I hope not. While my other classes seemed to go OK, my problem is still the ¾ group (I fear this will become a familiar refrain). I had them doing group work on the slave stories. It was a little impromptu, but I thought that if they were able to work together, they might be able to get more done. Several of the groups (the girls) asked if they could work out in the hall (because of the noise). Although I felt like it was a personal defeat, as if they were saying they didn't think I would ever gain control of the class, I agreed. Partially this was because I agreed that it was loud in the room (and they might be right about my chances of getting control), and partly because I thought they might actually get something done when isolated. It turned out to only work so-so. I got reports back from each group, but they were neither as extensive nor as good as I would have liked. Most groups, rather than sharing ideas, simply divided up the work, so that each one had to do less. Not what I was aiming for. I'll have to refine the process before I try it again (at least with this class). In the rest of the classes we watched the end of "Glory" despite the problems that seem to be growing with it. I just got word that one of the local news-rags, whose editor apparently hates the school because it screwed her out of a printing contract, might do a story about the situation. That's just what I need, three weeks into a new job—a negative article in the newspaper. Oh well, I knew there could be trouble, I just didn't think it would snowball like this. Live and learn. Besides, I must admit that I'm a little amused by the whole thing, provided it doesn't get any worse.

Not well as it turned out. Here is what happened. Mr. Cary had to write a letter to the Board of Education about the movie situation, so that they didn't have to read about it in the paper first. It was a wonderful letter, and I couldn't have asked for a better defense. The PTA meeting went fine, although it was one of the most boring things I have ever been to. Mrs. Sullivan, who was the parent who had called Cary to tell him that she didn't have a problem with the movie, but that other parents might, was there, and I could see right away that she was a real busy-body, although whether it was of the meddling type, or the interfering type, I couldn't tell. In any case, the article came out today, and it wasn't that bad. My name wasn't even mentioned, and the whole thing came off (at least the way I saw it) as an innocent mistake that wasn't a real problem. They even mentioned my disclaimer, of not having to watch the film. So I think the whole thing is going to blow over, though I did get a message to call one of my students' (and advisees') parents, so that might be about this as well. In any case, the open house is Monday, so we'll see if it comes up there, and if not, I think the issue will be more or less dead. So, on to bigger and better things. Everyone has been working on the "Glory" assignment, and I've never heard so much bitching in my life. I even had some parents come in and talk to me about it, though they were all nice, and there was no problem. I finally had to model what I wanted with the students, taking one of the characters and looking at his own motivation, and how one could find such a thing in the film. I'm a little worried that the assignment is too difficult for these kids, but I want to keep my expectations high, so I'm going ahead with it. But I think I should start to focus on things that are a little more concrete for a while, just to bring the kids' confidence back up.

OPEN HOUSE TONIGHT! So far I've had the advisory meeting, and I thought it went very well. About 2/3 of my advisees' parents came, and there was no hostility, yet. We'll see how the evening progresses. I managed to explain everything we've done in perfect context and I think I addressed some of the concerns parents might have without their even needing to voice them.

Well… I'm finding that most of these kids aren't quite as developed as I thought. They seem to have a problem with abstract ideas, at least most of them. I was hoping to do a lot with ideas and connections, but perhaps I overestimated them. I'm going to have to get a little more concrete. This presents a whole new set of problems. How do I make the information interesting when I'm not even teaching the stuff *I'm* interested in? It's bad enough that I have to do US history, which is interesting enough, but not as good as world, but to have to do it based on facts, not necessarily the more interesting ideas. What will be my source of passion? I've known all along that I'm more interested in the material than the kids, teaching history, not history students, as the saying goes, but I'm afraid I just won't enjoy anything here if I'm forced to teach **down** to kids who just are incapable of approaching things in a way that interests me. I've begun to have thoughts about trying to transfer to the high school (even fleeting ones about leaving the business). I don't mean to sound morbid, and it's not as bad as this, but I'm really beginning to get frustrated. Another thing along the same line—I was unable to get *Ender's Game* approved as an English book. I couldn't believe it! All because the word "bastard" appears twice, and there is one reference to "I'll cut off your balls" (admittedly that phrase was questionable). I mean, for God's sake, the book was written by a devout Mormon (if there's a stiffer bunch of people, I don't know about them).

Chapter Three

STEPHEN'S LETTER OF RESIGNATION

Dr. Charles Ebbetino
Superintendent
Shoreham-Wading River School System

Dear Dr. Ebbetino,

This is to inform you of my reluctant resignation from my position in the Shoreham-Wading River School District effective February 1, 1998. However, before I leave, I would like to comment on some of the circumstances that have led me to this point.

First, there is my AOL profile. Of the problems that I had here in Shoreham, I must admit this is the most bizarre and regrettable. I wrote the profile as a joke back when I was still in school. Member profiles are rarely taken seriously, even on AOL, and I was just having fun with some friends of mine, one of whom is now an engineer, another a lawyer.

We all wrote profiles that tweaked our new professions, had a few laughs, and promptly forgot about it. That it would come back to haunt me in such a way was something I never even imagined. I still find it hard to believe that so many took this silly little document seriously. But I am certainly sorry for any anxiety it might have caused to parents.

Second, there were concerns about my grading system. While it is true that I gave very few A's during the first month and a half of school, I do not see why this should have been a problem. In these days of complaints that our students do not do well enough in school, holding them to a higher standard is one way to encourage them to push their own limits. In addition, I came into this system without much experience in the middle school, especially a middle school like this one. For this reason, it was relatively easy to get a B from me, and much harder to earn an A. I can say, in defense of this policy, is that it has worked for me in the past, and that the work I was getting from the students at the end of my tenure was considerably improved from the stuff I was getting at the beginning.

Next, there was the film, "Glory." I guess I should have realized, from the reaction to the movie, that this was a system in which I would have to be careful. I thought, and still think, that it is a wonderful, powerful film about the nature of courage and war, and I still encourage everyone to see it. Although I did not know about the policy of getting parental permission, I did offer every student the chance to opt out of the movie with no prejudice, something no student took advantage of. In addition, from what I understand, the entire 8th grade went to see the movie when it first came out, so it can hardly be called inappropriate for the age group. I'm sorry I did an end run around school policy, but I hardly think anyone was harmed by the viewing of such an epic event in our country's history.

Finally, there is the classroom itself. There were complaints about the noise, about the lack of direction, and about the use of some words that, in other circumstances, would be reprehensible. It is true that I had a loud class, sometimes too loud. I like to have a classroom in which students feel comfortable to express their opinions, indeed to change their opinions in the face of evidence they had not seen before. If they disagree with something I say, I want them to feel free to question me about it. And I want them to interact with each other. All of these things help students to deepen their understanding and connection to the events they study. However, having such a classroom is a delicate balancing act, as students sometimes have a tendency to lose focus. It takes a while to establish the right balance in such a classroom between instruction, of whatever form, and student activities, and I had not yet reached such an equilibrium. I'm sorry I did not get a chance to finish. With regard to the language in the classroom, especially the use of the "N" word, it was used in the context of reading primary documents written by slaves, about being slaves, documents I obtained from the school. The "N" word was commonplace back then, without most of the negative connotations that it has since acquired and, as such, appeared in the stories. To not use it myself seemed disingenuous, taking something away from the people writing these stories, by imposing our own standards on their language. I did inform the students of the circumstances surrounding the use of the word, that it was unacceptable to use it today, and that its meaning has changed over time. I thought that was enough. Apparently I was wrong.

In conclusion, let me just say that I am very sorry things didn't work out here in Shoreham. When I packed up my life to move to Shoreham, on the spur of the moment, I looked forward to working in a system in which parents were more involved, in which students cared about learning and doing well. The fact that it was these same circumstances that led to my current situation is an irony not lost on me. I wish nothing but

the best for the system, Dr. Bell, and especially the students who have had to deal with
these unfortunate events.

Sincerely,
Stephen Cohen

Shoreham Advice: (My letter to Steve)

Some thoughts on our conversation yesterday.
I wouldn't give up on teaching so quickly.
You have a specialized education and you
will have passed a state license exam. There
are many benefits to the profession. Believe
me, there is plenty of bull shit everywhere in
life. We all have to learn how to cope. As for
your deficiencies in discipline—you can learn
discipline (which you didn't get much of last
year in Providence jumping around to different classes) by assistance gained in training,
in classes, tips from older teachers. It's like
a game of squash. When you're behind, you
learn to change your strategy.

To repeat some of my comments. You should
neither expect nor try to have a class love you.
You're not their parent but their teacher. That
doesn't mean that love doesn't follow. But it's
earned by a combination of fairness, work,
and discipline. By respect for one another.

Also, you have to be aware of cues you

unwittingly send the class. A purple shirt and red tie says: "Hey, I'm unique, a character, liberal, and I invite your own creative (eccentric) behavior." It's like the red cape of a matador to a bull; people's behavior is affected by color. And clothes don't make the inner man. You don't have to announce your uniqueness by dress. A more neutral dress code, even if it is conservative (preppie) doesn't make you any the less creative. It also keeps them guessing as to who and what you are. At the other extreme, it's why the army shaves the head of their recruits and everyone wears khaki. That is an extreme, even ideological, way of leveling everyone and thereby controlling them, a rather onerous form of discipline.

To repeat. I think it's too early to ditch teaching. You can always explore other job venues but it's easier to do it while you have a job as a teacher. You have all summer available to look. You have to earn your own way right now! And you must, for your own self esteem. At this stage I can provide a sounding board for you and give you an opinion. You have to deal with your future, responsibly, by yourself, and I think you can do it. You can resurrect yourself but it's going to require plenty of self-discipline and courage. And you can't waste time. Although I have urged you to pray, don't expect any divine assistance from either God or father. Treat Shoreham as a wakeup call but also as an aberration and don't let it get you down.

Love you,
Dad

The School Committee gave Stephen an administrative job downtown, until January. He made friends there with the assistant superintendent of schools, who recommended him to a friend, who hired for The American Schools in foreign countries. Steve got his resume back in the mail. He didn't want to return to substitute teaching, although that would have been an option. In February he went to Boston for an interview with the Director of the American School in Nicaragua. They offered him a job later that day.

I was vacationing in London when he called to ask my advice—should he take the job? No warning flags penetrated my jet-lagged brain. He would be teaching advanced placement American and European History to students who were mostly headed to college in the United States. "Yes," I said, happy he had found an opportunity so quickly.

PART SIX
To Nicaragua

Saren encounters the Qualin on the Golian Highlands. This is his first encounter with humanity, and he is fascinated by their freedom of action and the amusing way they have developed without a God to call their own. He sets up among a dense cluster of Qualin and organizes them to chronicle the Qualin way of life. At first the shamen are suspicious of Saren, but when he recognizes their knowledge and puts them in corresponding positions of power in the new community, they relent and help him wholeheartedly. Saren teaches them how to domesticate animals and plants and how to settle down in communities. He sends emissaries from this new community of learning far and wide to learn of the rest of the Qualin. In the temples of Saren that arise all across the Highlands, it is well known that all are welcome.

—*The History of Lathrim*

MANAGUA, NICARAGUA

Dear New Teachers:

Are you packed yet? We are awaiting your arrival in Managua and at the American Nicaraguan School.

Enclosed you will find your tickets and flight itinerary.

Here are some tips you may choose to follow in deciding what to bring.

> —Cool clothes for very hot weather. Shorts may be worn to school, but they must be knee length. Jeans are not allowed. Nice sandals are acceptable, but no beach shoes. We recommend you bring at least one fairly formal outfit or suit. Swimsuits and beachwear are very practical for weekends and vacations. You may also want to bring clothes hangers.

> —Bring what you can't or don't want to live without. Things such as books, music, CD player, TV, VCR, camera, film, alarm clock (with battery backup), etc.

> —Flashlights and candles for when the lights go out (occasionally). Floor lamps if you wish, as all lighting here is overhead. Lamps here are quite costly.

> —Towels, sheets, and pillows. You will need

queen-size as well as twin sheets.

–If you have a particular taste in personal items such as shampoo, soap, toothpaste, deodorant, etc., bring them with you. Although these items are easily found at the local market, there is not necessarily the variety of brands we are accustomed to in the States. Some of these things may also cost more here.

–If you have special medical needs or medications, please make sure you are supplied for at least six months. Many medications are available here, but you want to be sure.

The school provides coffee makers, toaster ovens, dishes and silverware for four, pots and pans, one telephone, and basic furniture. During your first week here, we will be going to the local market where you can purchase basic household items (fans, blenders, etc...) at reasonable prices.

Bring a sense of humor and adventure, patience, and an open mind. Nicaragua is a beautiful country with warm people, sunny beaches, spectacular lakes, tropical rainforests, and volcanoes.

Once again, we anxiously await your arrival here in sunny Managua.

See you on July 27.

Chapter One

July 27, 1998 (Monday)

Well, here I am on my way to Houston, in route to Managua. So far things have gone as smoothly as I could have hoped, considering how late I got started on everything (a habit I really have to get out of). Kinneson's safe in the belly of this beast in his dog crate and hopefully untroubled by anything more than my absence. Getting him squared away was my biggest headache, and I'm extremely relieved that it seems to have gone off without a hitch. In any case, enough about the preparations for the journey. Since I'm going to be meeting up with other teachers in Houston, I thought I'd get some thoughts down about what I'm getting myself into.

Overall, I have to say that I'm quite excited about the journey ahead, although that has been, I think, my feeling before and things have turned out to be, shall we say, somewhat less than expected. In any case, I simply don't know enough about the new school and situation to have strong feelings one way or the other. I have to say that I'm looking forward to teaching highly motivated high school students, as opposed to those middle school brats (said only half in jest). I know I want to stress writing again; the question becomes how to do it without running into the complaints about too much work. One mitigating factor might be the fact that I'll be a little more flexible on grades, as well as making it a little clearer about what my expectations are. I know that was a problem in Long Island, but it's hard to impose firm standards and still encourage creativity. I know I would have gotten a lot less out of high school if I hadn't been able to have fun with my papers (of course that only semi-served me in college). Also, I really want to see what I can do about some cross-pollination with English and maybe even Science. I think there should be opportunities to do that. And it gets me to my next goal—good relations with the other teachers and administration. I know I've gotten off to a bit of a bad start with the latter because of my tardiness. In any case, being a little more social at school should yield dividends.

Now, on to the other aspect of this whole thing that is hanging over my head like a Damoclean Sword—the fact that I'm moving to Nicaragua for all this. All right—let's go through the basics first, in descending order of terror. First—food—I know I'll have to change my eating habits, but to what degree and how will I cope? I have to say that really has me stumped. Since I've basically had my own way for so long, it will certainly be a big adjustment to change anything. All I can say is that I'm willing to be at least a little flexible (though I'm not sure my palate will necessarily agree). Second—a foreign language. There's two ways to go. I might become somewhat of a hermit. That's certainly one way to go, I just hope I don't end up choosing it. Or I can stumble my way through Spanish for two years, hoping something of what I spent years learning will seep back into my frontal lobe and that my feelings about my own ability with languages is ripped asunder upon the reefs of immersion. If I don't come back with at least a passing knowledge of Spanish, it will be a darn shame. But this segues nicely into the third, and in some ways most important, thing—I've got to be more social. Whether it's in school, or out, I've GOT to at least try to be more social. I know that the food thing and the language thing are both wonderful excuses as inhibitors, but that's all they are, and I've got to get past them. This is the best opportunity I've had since college to forge new friendships, and I should take advantage of it.

OK—now we're on our way to Managua. Thought I'd throw in a few more things before the battery on this thing begins to wind down. I met a couple of the other new teachers, which gives me something of an idea what to expect. They're both young (20s), with little or no teaching experience, and they don't seem any readier for this whole thing than I do. Their names are Will, from Chicago, and Crystelle, from Boston. Don't know that much more about them, but they seem nice (in the same way anyone who might share a scary experience with you might seem nice). We'll have to see what else develops when we get there. I did hear that the apartments we're supposed to get are supposedly OK (but no air conditioning— like that was likely). Thank God I made a fuss about getting Kinneson on the plane—he almost didn't make it.

All right, it's still the first day, but now I'm in Nicaragua. I'm about to go to sleep in my apartment which is—25 minutes off campus!! Now I have to rely on people to get me to and from work every day, as well as wasting an hour out of the day commuting. Christ, this is not what I signed up for. Also, let's see, apparently you can't get on the Internet from here (DAMN DAMN DAMN!!!), there's no fan in my room (of course there's an overhead fan in every other room, go figure), AND AND AND to top it all off—none of our luggage got here (they're now saying it might get here tomorrow). We'll see. In any case, I'm not at all happy about any of this. Plus, Kinneson is wheezing away like an out-of-control locomotive. I'll probably have to do something about that before long. All right, enough for now, I'm going to bed (by the way—it's not all bad, I'll talk about the positives tomorrow—but right now I just want to wallow.

July 28, 1998 (Tuesday):

Well, here we are, Nicaragua, day two. Met more teachers today. I'm surprised at how many local teachers they hire. Got something of my class schedule. There are two sections of AP European History, and they both seem to be full. We'll have to see about that. I'll be real pissed if they expect me to teach three APs and another class, especially when they promised two and one, and the AP classes weren't supposed to be more than 12 or so. Of course, at least I'm teaching in my area, something not everyone can say. In any case, they sure didn't give us much to go on academically yet; hopefully that will change tomorrow or the next day. Now, let's see what else. I met the principal and asst. principal of the secondary school. They both seemed OK, at least at first glance. We'll have to see how they are when the shit hits the fan (which it hopefully won't). Saw my classroom, pretty much what I'd expected (though I do have a Dry Erase board, somewhat surprisingly).

Went to the market, where I was surprised by two things— that they had many items, or the equivalent to what there is in the US, and that things were so goddamn expensive. I spent 80 bucks, and barely got anything worth mentioning. So much for the low cost of living. This reminds me—they paid up today, at least in the local currency. Got about 2000 córdoba (cords). This is about $200. Spent a lot already, so I'm glad we're getting paid again at the end of the week (I forgot our contract starts at the beginning of July, so we're already getting our first month's salary—YEA. Managua has relatively broad streets, separated by grassy dividers, and shacks everywhere along the road. Traffic is pretty crazy. I'm now waiting to go out to dinner at Mary Ellen's, the director's house. I'm still not happy at all about living so far off campus and I'm PISSED about the Internet thing, but we'll have to see what happens with time. I almost electrocuted myself today in the shower. Boy, they've got a fun set-up there. Still no word on the bags. Hope they come tonight.

I'm home from the dinner party now. And I'm as close to panic as I have ever been as a teacher. I talked to the teacher who used to do the APs and found out some jarring facts. First—the European History covers from the Renaissance to the present day. All the books I brought are for long before that (and it happens to be my area of expertise). Second, and even worse, I can't believe the schedule she laid out. My GOD! "Prepare a ninety-minute lecture for every class" was the gist of her advice. "And make sure it's not on the stuff in the book; they should already get that on their own." And the summer reading list they had to do, everything from *The Prince* to *Mein Kampf* (hell, I haven't read half the stuff). And that's just for the European class. I still have to think about the American History, as well as the damn Civics class. Like I said, I'm in a panic. What the hell am I going to do???? I don't like anything about this. And, frankly, I wasn't real thrilled with Mary Ellen either. She seemed rather harsh and humorless. Now, it is true that she recently lost her husband, the effect of which I can't even begin to imagine, but this seems separate and ingrained. I sure hope I don't become like that. By the way, I think my panic was beginning to show, various people came up to me and asked me if I was OK. I can't remember the last time that happened. I'm usually so good at concealing my emotions that I must be in worse shape than I suspected for it to be that obvious. In any case, I went to Gary (guidance/scheduling) whose role here I'm still not real sure about, and he reassured me a bit with the promise of more tomorrow when we meet, but I just don't know. I'm not looking forward to any of this. In any case, I'm going to relax with a bit of Civ before I go to bed, to start the whole thing over again. Still no sign of the luggage.

July 29, 1998 (Wednesday):

Well, today was a whole lot of nothing. Had meetings with the guidance counselors in the morning and with the principal later. Blah, blah, blah. Went over the handbooks, lots of common-sense stuff. Had no time to work in the classrooms, but met some more teachers. Later, went to the market and got a boom box and some clothes. (Oh yeah—the luggage still isn't here—but Continental told us they'd reimburse us for $100 worth of stuff we needed to get by.) Got some shirts, another pillow, two towels, and some sheets, all of which was criminally expensive (well, not the shirts, they were cheap as hell—$8 each. New rule: if you plug it in, it's god-awful expensive. If you put it on, it's cheap (unless it had to be imported, then it's back to being god-awful expensive), but that's a lot easier to take when it's free. Later, went to a dinner party at one of the teachers' houses—it was actually nice (at least more than I was expecting).

July 30, 1998 (Thursday):

Well, nothing much has changed. I'm still nervous about the classes, though it is still getting easier. I'm hoping to have some fun in the civics class, as that is the only one that has no fixed standard. I spent a lot of the day going through the materials at hand. Boy, the book for the European History class is the most boring thing I have ever seen in my entire life. Very few pictures and those in black and white. Lots of dry text and nothing to bring the events alive. I guess my biggest concern right now is that I feel under- (or even un-) prepared for the classes, and there don't seem to be the materials necessary to get prepared available anywhere around here. I'm going to have to rely heavily on the other teachers, especially the ones who taught these classes before. That will be a new experience, and one I'm not thrilled about. I know that I have to do a better job of working with the rest of the teachers than I did before, but I hate coming to them as a supplicant, needing everything from them.

The good news is that the luggage finally arrived. (YEA!!!) I even got unpacked. I did have to go to customs to get my VCR (they apparently think that anyone who brings some-thing electronic into the country wants to sell it), and they stamped my passport so that I can't, theoretically, bring any-thing electronic into the country for six months, but we'll see about that. At least I got my stuff. Will and Crystelle still are waiting for things (they were supposed to be at customs but, after waiting around for a few hours, we decided to get out of there). In any case, it's nice to have some stuff to play with now. Oh, and one of the reasons I feel better about things is that my books got here, and some of them might prove useful after all.

I was afraid that I had brought all the ancient stuff and left behind anything I might use, but no—I do have some things to apply. And, most importantly, the Speilvogel text goes up to 1715, so that should last until the next volume gets here. In any case, we have a beach day tomorrow, so I probably won't get much done, but with the weekend coming up, and no class on Monday, I should be able to prepare enough to get through.

July 31, 1998 (Friday):

Not much to say today. Went to the beach and to a nature preserve with the rest of the group. Got a bit sunburned, but it could have been much worse. Had a nice, relaxing time. I'm feeling better about the classes, but that might just be because I've managed to put them out of my mind for the time being. I have to start buckling down soon (but not now). Talked a bit more to Mrs. Burgess (the one who taught the World History class before). Have you ever met a person who is just on a different wavelength from you? It's not that you dislike them, or that there's anything wrong with them, you just don't connect well together. That's how it is between me and Mrs. Burgess. I just felt uncomfortable around her. Oh, well. In any case, it's nice to have my stuff here and put away. I got through about half of *Lucifer's Hammer*, enjoying it all the way. It was the first time I fell into my old pattern of reading in social situations (well, I did bring *The Economist* to the customs house, but that doesn't count). I've been trying to be social, but it really is a chore. I feel so much more comfortable, and involved, when I'm reading. Sigh. I also tried to eat some different food, but that just didn't work either, and I'm feeling a bit queasy now. Oh, and I haven't taken a dump since I moved here (five days and counting). Isn't it ironic, Kinneson adapted to the new location and food in a day or two, and now he's regular as clockwork, but my system has shut down completely. I've been taking vitamins regularly, so there's nothing wrong with my diet (I've actually been eating quite like I always did, though less). Hope my system finally decides to accept this is home now—and lets go (though I am saving money on toilet paper). But I'm gonna go away now.

August 1, 1998 (Saturday):

Woke up in agony from my feet. Who knew that burning the top of your feet could destroy your ability to walk? It's funny, lying or sitting down there's no problem, and once I get going walking isn't such a problem. But standing in place is impossible, absolute agony. Had to go to the pool party at Mary Ellen's, didn't think I would make it through the whole thing. Actually it was kind of fun, at least parts were. Lots of people got drunk and loosened up, which is always a trip. It rained a lot, so no one went swimming, but they found other ways to entertain themselves. I just sat there listening to various conversations. Oh, I met the other history teachers at the high school—they seemed very nice and helpful. Hopefully we'll make a good team (with or without Mrs. Burgess). Also managed to get some lotion for my feet there, as well as some tea bags (supposedly the tannin in tea is good for burns—don't know, but I'll try tomorrow).

Let's see what else. God, my new (old) TV. It seems to work OK, but nothing special (hey—what would you want for $80 around here). Also, I found the biggest spider I've ever seen in my bathroom. Because of the feet I was loathe to take it on, so I just shut the door and hope it will go away the same way it came (however that is). It's a shame too, because I was going in there to try to take a dump, it felt possible. Oh, well—have to wait another day. Hopefully I'll have success then. Oh, there is one thing that I want to comment on that's struck me as kind of funny—time seems to move rather slowly here. I don't mean that in any kind of cliché way, and it's not that I seem to get more done in a given amount of time, it's just that time itself seems to move more slowly. Or maybe it's just that I'm noticing the passage of time more down here than I realize. Who knows? In any case, I finished *Lucifer's Hammer* (there goes one of my precious books). It was worth bringing. Lots of fun and well put together. Tomorrow I really have to do some work on the classes. Get ready for the big day Tuesday (hope my feet are better by then).

August 2, 1998 (Sunday):

OK, technically it's the morning of the 3rd and I'm already at school. God, here I am, classes not even started yet, and I'm already falling behind. Got to do better. Speaking of got to do better, I didn't get all that much done yesterday either. I got an idea of what I have to work with for the American History class, as far as my own books, and that helped to alleviate some of the anxiety. The civics class I'm less sure of. I don't really know what I'm going to be doing there yet. Obviously something on constitutionalism, and I'd like to be able to have the class set up its own constitution, but we'll have to see about the schedule, and that still leaves a whole lot of time to fill up. Have to talk to some of the other teachers about the class. In any case, I want to do more role-playing and having fun there. For the US History, I found that the Zinn, the Davis, and the Princeton Review books have enough different and more information to help fill in some of the gaps, enough to make

198

me look like I know more than I do. I did think about structure a little this morning. The fact is the amount of material, and the test itself, sort of dictates the structure. We have to get through about 23 chapters by Christmas, which works out to two classes a chapter. That isn't much (I think the numbers are about the same for the World History classes). I'm figuring on a quiz for every chapter, a test for every few chapters (two or three), and written assignments on those days that there isn't either. I also had an idea about grading that might make things easier, and make the kids a little happier with the system. Since the AP itself doesn't require a perfect score to pass, I'll do something similar; in other words, scale up the wazoo. I figure that there will be enough opportunities in class to see how everyone is doing, that I don't need to kill them on the tests; the AP itself will do that. As we get closer and closer to the test, I'll start moving things more and more in parallel to the test, so that the kids are truly ready when the test rolls around.

August 3, 1998 (Monday):

Well, it's still the same day but my mood has changed so completely that I feel quite justified in calling this a new session. That new feeling—utter frustration. This place is really beginning to get on my nerves. First of all, the textbook for the AP American History class isn't here at all, and no one is sure when it might come. Second, there are in fact only 20 of the European History books (a piss-poor book to begin with), not even enough for one class. I'm beginning to feel less and less guilt about working to drive kids out of these classes. Let's see, what else...There are no maps in this whole damn school (I already said the library was awful, didn't I?). Oh, and this isn't a big thing, but jeez, they could have told us before—the schedule for tomorrow is a Tuesday schedule, not a first day one, so I brought the wrong books in here to prepare with. On the one hand, that's good, because I only have to worry about the European History class tomorrow, but on the other hand, I wish I'd known, so I'd have something to do here in school today. The whole thing is just so damn disorganized. Also, I have no idea what to do in the civics class, and Annette Burgess is so busy running around she can't help me with anything. In other words—**FRUSTRATION** (it doesn't help that my feet are still killing me, though a little less than yesterday—just as the luggage saga ended, now we have the feet saga. Maybe that's what this whole experience will be like—one crisis after another). OK, maybe I'm going a bit overboard now, but Christ, these are AP classes—college freshman classes—and there is a test looming ahead, a test over which I have no control— **AND THEY HAVEN'T GIVEN ME THE MINIMAL EQUIPMENT NECESSARY TO DO MY JOB.** I'm tired of bitching and moaning, I have to get something done.

August 4, 1998 (Tuesday):

Today was it, my first teaching day here. So let me sum up the experience so far. Overall, my classes were good. Though they were large, they were already much better behaved than the kids in Long Island. Part of that was I think I did a better job of controlling the classroom and setting a good tone right from the start. Part of it was just that I scared the kids with the work they are going to have to do. I was a little worried about the second class because the first (both were the European AP classes) was more of a homeroom than an actual class, so we didn't get that much work done. I didn't want the other class to get too far ahead on the first day, so we had to find things to do, to pass the time, without really doing anything. I ended up spending more time talking about the makeup of the class, and then we started Greece, and I ended up going with the old standby of using an inanimate object (in this case, a pencil sharpener) to prove that we have no free will. Several of the kids seemed to get into that, and it ended up taking enough time so that I was able to finish up class without a problem. In any case, I hope I did enough to scare some of the kids off; the classes are still way too big (**AND WE NEED BOOKS!!**).

August 5, 1998 (Wednesday):

Well, today I saw the other half of my classes. Again, I was quite impressed by them. The US History class was good, and we actually got somewhere, as I was able to talk them through the 14th century and we got started on the 15th. We got up through the Portuguese and are poised to start on the Spanish. That's good, because I hope to at least get to the early English settlements by the end of class Friday, so that we have something I can test them on Tuesday (First Quiz! Yea!). Boy, I hope some of them drop the class soon—it's WAY too big. The civics class was interesting. We got started on this whole constitution thing, and it went fairly well, though not quite as well as I might have hoped (that's probably my fault—not quite organized enough yet). There are some VERY sharp students in that class, one especially, who raised the point at the end of the class that we hadn't really done anything radical. I hadn't even thought about things from that perspective, so it gave me something to think about. What is it—trust issues? (With me or with the other students?) Inability to see beyond the obvious? A desire not to see things change? I'll want to bring this up again Friday. In any case, it was one of the most interesting comments I've ever received from a student. I'll have to keep an eye on her. If it proves to be a not atypical remark, it tells me I'm dealing with someone who's not only intelligent, but confident in their intelligence, and able to look at things in more than one way. Reminds me a little of myself (I'm not sure who's being flattered, or insulted, there). In any case—we'll see what happens Friday.

August 6, 1998 (Thursday):

Well, here we go. My feet are feeling better, so I guess that's the signal for something else to go wrong (crisis, to crisis, to crisis—remember). And it did—I'm losing my voice. Yesterday afternoon it started to get bad, and this morning it sounds terrible. I gargled with salt water last night, which did make it feel better. I've even been taking these Halls cough drops (YUCK!), which, again, made it feel better, but that hasn't improved the quality of my speech. I was beginning to feel a little desperate—then I remembered my Linwood Thompson. Ended up showing both the AP European classes his lecture on the Middle Ages. It did a more-than-adequate job of covering the subject. Then I gave them a break and then filled in some of the blanks on my own—especially on the way the peasant of the medieval world thought. It seemed to go over OK, except for a few kids who told me they were dropping the class, but still had to come today. Gary Fernandez apparently told them to stick around for a week. But what good is that doing anyone?

• • •

My once-a-week call became his regular line of communication with home. After conversing for an hour, he and I hated to hang up—such a wistful sound in his voice to prolong the conversation, such love in my heart for my son, who was managing to do such good work.

"I'm lucky they gave me an apartment outside of town," Steve had commented. "It's a higher elevation and there are fewer mosquitoes up here." He thought his cowboy boots saved him because they covered his exposed ankles.

In the fall of 1998, Hurricane Mitch hit Central America.

"It's been raining here for two weeks solid," Steve said on my weekly long-distance call. Widespread flooding caused mudslides and thousands died, including the teenage son of the lower school principal, who had driven into a large puddle in the road only to have his car quickly flooded and swept away.

"Don't worry, Dad," Steve had said.

Chapter Two

It was Nicaragua's Independence Day, the beginning of Steve's second year when we visited him, and school was closed for a two-day holiday. Cursed with bad luck, Nicaragua had been robbed of its resources by a corrupt dictator, who embezzled funds devoted to rebuilding after a major earthquake. Catastrophic civil war followed and periodic epidemics of dengue fever.

If there was a center to Managua, it might have been the InterContinental Hotel. As we circled around, catching a glimpse now and then of its pyramid shape, it vanished behind trees. We were lost and came to a vacant square. The huge ghost of a cathedral stood there, its roof caved in, windows shattered by the earthquake. A magnificent building—why had it not been rebuilt? Children came over to our car and offered sliced fruit for sale, candy, the daily newspaper. At each traffic light, a competition occurred among other children to wash our windshield. Steve always gave them a small tip. I let my sense of direction take over and guided Steve, by instinct, to the rear of the hotel where we circled just one more time up to the entrance.

The *Inter*, as Steve called it affectionately, was functional enough. Built in a flying-buttress style out of concrete, it had survived the earthquake, one of few large buildings to do so. It had been the hangout for journalists covering the Civil War. Armed private guards strolled outside the entrance and in the lobby. Our room had a view in back towards the big statue on the hill, a monument and park honoring Augusto César Sandino, General of the Free Men, who had led the guerrilla war in 1927 from his base in the mountains to the north. From a distance it looked enormous, but on closer inspection it was a sort of sham figure made of flat steel plate, like a cardboard cutout hero. A tin-shack neighborhood began immediately at the confluence of hotel and park, with barbed-wire fence separating it from a military post guarding the monument. In the hotel shop, Steve bought a T-shirt printed with the slogan "I survived Hurricane Mitch." He joined us for an early dinner at the hotel, indulging in an Argentinean beefsteak, then left to take his dog for a walk. He'd pick us up midmorning.

Our beds were flat and hard as a board, the generic *Inter*-bed in Managua, nothing you could do about it. The next morning, however, we changed our room to one with a view over the busy, scrambling city.

Steve looked good and he had quite recovered from the shock of his dismissal that wasn't a dismissal. At the end of last year, he'd had several students in each class pass their AP exam in American and European History. He knew that with second-year experience and an established curriculum, he'd do even better. His classes were stimulating and, while we couldn't see him in action because of the holiday, he felt there was plenty of time for the school to reverse itself by June.

We got the guided tour, first to Steve's old apartment up a hill, almost ten kilometers outside the city, green vegetation everywhere, and traffic that Steve whistled confidently through like a Grand Prix race driver. I had white knuckles by the time we reached his first digs. He turned in towards the gate and a guard opened it. The stone walls were topped with circular barbed wire. Inside was a community of small buildings, perhaps eight apartments with corrugated rooftops. He navigated his car between them to his former residence, locked for the holiday weekend. We wanted to see inside of one.

"Maybe Jonathan is still here. All my other friends have left for a place closer to school except Jon. He gave me most of my rides last year." The Nicaraguan buses were crowded and not very dependable. They were mostly old yellow school buses from the US, owned by a cartel. To get to school on time for 7:00 a.m., Steve had to hitch a ride. By the end of June, only Jon was left with his pickup truck, with Steve riding in the rear like an itinerant farm worker, grateful for the lift.

In fact, Jon was still around for the weekend. Steve proudly introduced us to the young biology teacher. His shy Nicaraguan bride stayed in another room of the small apartment until Jon insisted she come out to meet us. They were doing their weekend chores with a college football game playing on TV. I thanked him for helping Steve last semester. "We stick together," he said.

Steve's current apartment was a couple of kilometers closer to town, rented from a retired American, also married to a Nicaraguan woman. I thought of the old calypso tune: "If you want to be happy for the rest of your life, never make a pretty woman your wife." Steve was ready for a helpmate, a woman who could balance that lopsided intelligence of his with a practical touch. Once he got planted in the American school system, I was sure *she'd* find *him*.

His apartment was spacious and the neatest Steve ever had, thanks to his once-a-week housekeeper who washed his clothes in a barrel outside and hung them on a line. Proud of his space, Steve showed us around the two-and-a-half rooms, a bedroom-study with all his books, a large bathroom, and a living room-kitchen. Kinneson greeted us with howls and whining just like old times.

"Do you think he remembers us?" I asked.

"Of course. He's saying hello to you."

Once a small pottery factory, there were lots of overhead plugs to run each potter's wheel. Steve's TV and electronic equipment were connected by electric cords hanging from the ceiling. His recent purchases of native pottery, from various markets around Managua, were brightly colored, animistic forms that fit in perfectly. We waited while he took Kinneson for a walk and then we left his barbed-wire compound. "That's a Nicaraguan fence," Steve joked. Managua sprawled like a Los Angeles on the shores of a brown lake in which nothing lived. It must have once been a beautiful land before it became a city divided into zones of poverty.

"Squalor starts one hundred yards off the highway," observed Steve on the way to The American School.

"What would you call this?" I asked. Goats were chewing on household garbage piled by the roadside.

"Maybe just degradation. Everyone hopes the IMF will forgive all Nicaraguan debt but no one is sure if the politicians would use the payments to rebuild the infrastructure. There are twenty thousand people ahead of me just waiting for a direct telephone connection."

Everyone had abandoned The American School for the long vacation weekend, some to the Pacific coast, others to the Corn Islands offshore in the Caribbean or to Costa Rica. We parked and he led us to his classroom, past rows of neat buildings on a large campus, relatively new since the earthquake. His room had a glass wall and an open feeling. School messages were tacked on bulletin boards, a gardener watered plants, shade trees dotted the grounds leading to a soccer field and basketball courts. One of his friends was playing basketball with his 'novia,' an attractive Nicaraguan woman. Steve introduced us, but I don't remember his name. He taught history in the classroom next to Steve.

"He's a bit of a loner," Steve said. "We get along fine."

Huembes Market had a unique Nicaraguan quality, and if any place were the center of Managua, I think Huembes could claim the distinction. "Here is where I get my hair cut...three dollars." When Steve first told me about Huembes I imagined someone clipping his hair in a large open-air market, but, in fact, it was just one shop of hundreds selling all the staples and sundries of daily living in a vast multi-roofed bazaar, in a space taking up perhaps several football fields. His barber had a very nice salon, indeed.

"And here's where I bought my last cowboy boots, forty-five dollars. What a bargain! It's packed in here during the week," Steve said. "Clothing and furniture is cheap, but anything that plugs in is expensive." It was Sunday in late afternoon and the crowds had thinned.

"They need to replace the Panama Canal," I said. "Reconnect through Lake Managua. That would jump-start the economy."

"There's always been talk of that and wouldn't you know Costa Rica claims they own the river connecting to the Caribbean that shares their common border. It really belongs to Nicaragua." Steve was partisan now in his politics.

We decided to give his old car a rest and hired a taxi the next day to take us to Masaya Park to see the volcano, then on to the old Spanish city of Granada, once the capital of Nicaragua. We chanced to see the same history teacher from school, getting out of his car to check into a small resident hotel. Stephen said he had another "novia" in Granada. "You should hang out with him," I replied.

I feel compelled to describe the minutiae of our days because it was the last time we spent with Steve. The luxury of enjoying one's children should never be taken lightly—each minute, in retrospect, so precious.

Heading south, the country had a rural beauty that belied its violent and transient natural forces. All it lacked were leaders who had the best interest of its people at heart. Up a winding road inside Volcan Masaya National Park we drove, past giant furrows of lava that had the appearance of a plowed field, the overwhelming remains of an eruption in the 1700s. Our hired car, a little taxi with its windows open for air conditioning, chugged up the road cut through sections of lava, parking at the top along the perimeter of the crater. Only one other car was there. The jagged crater edge peaked yet another 200 feet or so higher. Stairs climbed along the edge of the crater with a large cross installed at the very summit.

In a file we trudged up the steep steps, mounting to where a young couple stood arm-in-arm gazing at the magnificent view over the rolling countryside of green fields and crater lakes to another nearby still-active volcano. Although it hadn't exploded in over 200 years, a steady cloud of steam billowed from the depths of the Masaya crater. Its cone seemed narrow across, perhaps 200 meters, a young volcano with lots of energy left.

Steve stepped outside the guard rail, testing fate, to get a better look inside the crater. A sign warned against just such foolhardy acts. That didn't faze him. I watched from several steps away, my heart thumping as he poised one foot forward as if teetering on the toe and heel of his clunky boots, one foot behind him for a brake. He leaned over in slow motion. Perhaps 300 feet below, shades of incandescence glowed. I wanted to yell *Get back on the trail*, but not alarm him. Volcanic sand and stone beneath his feet. What if he slipped?

"Why did you do that?" I asked when we reached the parking lot. "There was no jumping in to save you."

"I know," he replied. "Relax. You're just being a dad."

We stopped for lunch at one of several verandah cafés overlooking a deep and expansive crater lake, very still and blue with not a single boat on it. A three-piece string band strolled over to serenade us.

"What do I tip them?" I asked Steve.

"Dad, if you were kidnapped and held ransom for three months, you'd probably ask, how much do I tip them when they exchanged you? The service was good." My son had a macabre sense of humor. "Tip whatever you like." Our driver, sensing my problem, said ten córdobas was customary.

From Masaya we continued on to Granada, which had a 17th-century Spanish colonial charm, centered on a large square planted with trees and tropical palms. Doors were open in a large cathedral, similar to the one in Managua, a service in progress. Out front, a horse-drawn hearse waited, covered with bouquets of flowers. The service had a lovely musical quality with tinkling bells in counterpoint to the organ. A young priest gave Communion.

Horse and wagon tours were available in the square, the horses skeletal, lean and worn like old leather. In Granada time flowed like congealed lava. We might still have been in that ancient century of its origin. On the edge of town, we fell behind another brightly covered hearse and a long line of mourners, until they took a turn and we gringos, always in a rush, sped back to Managua.

Once again, we reached the outskirts of the city without a center; empty lots and overgrown foundations, like an archeological site excavated and plundered by scavenger bands. At traffic lights, the same child-entrepreneurs offered to clean our window. Their voices pleaded; they were not easily discouraged. The cab driver turned on his washer-wipers and waved them off. Stephen muttered *Damn* in frustration, wanting to tip them all. A man in a wheelchair sat in the middle of a wide street like a traffic cop. A child attended him. Probably a victim of the Civil War, he held a white cloth poster in his lap with some political message about Ortega. Nearby a government building stood with Uzi-armed soldiers on guard.

"I have a feeling life here has been much worse," Steve replied, reading my mind.

"If I were to write about Managua," I observed, "I would describe it as how the world will end. It would be highly personal and probably highly inaccurate."

"If I wrote about it," replied Steve, "it would be impersonal and just as inaccurate."

The night before he died, he talked until the early morning hours with a new teacher he fancied. She was very pretty and somewhat reserved, and in his shy way, Steve had begun to court her. They discussed the great perplexing questions of existence that evening. When she went to bed, he started a file on his portable computer which he always carried with him, titled, "Liz," part of his Nicaraguan journal. He summarized their conversation as a list of hypothetical questions with few answers.

"Is survival the highest instinct?" they wondered that evening, as they peered together into the abyss.

• • •

Back home, we had returned from a concert Sunday afternoon. The message light on our telephone was blinking: two messages, one from George, who had gotten the call from the school in our absence. He was on Steve's emergency call list— his college roommate, as close to Steve as next of kin. The other, a woman's voice announcing who she was, Superintendent of The American-Nicaraguan School. "There is an emergency regarding your son, Stephen. Please call as soon as you get home."

I knew immediately when she answered the phone and began her charge to tell me as quickly as possible, extinguishing all hope; no road accident with blood and broken bones and Steve in the hospital. He had drowned in the Pacific Ocean, jumped off the rocks into the turbulent surf left over from a passing hurricane to save a dog. He was dead.

I was confused at first. Was it Steve's dog he had tried to rescue? No, he had left Kinneson home in Managua for the weekend in the care of a friend. It was the dog belonging to the family where they were staying. It had been swept off the rocks by a wave. The owner must have cried out, and Steve ran down the hill forsaking all caution, looking for a place to get across the rocks and into the water. He had little time to consider his options. Go or don't go. Jump in or let the animal be swept out to sea.

Stephen came to a strange land where he helped students who were eager to learn. It was gratifying to him. He touched too few lives during his brief teaching career and that is a shame.

CONDOLENCE LETTERS FROM HIS STUDENTS

I would like to take this opportunity to express my sincerest sympathy for your loss and also my gratitude for sharing your son's life with us. In the short time that I knew him, he managed to touch my life several times.

First of all, he was an example to me of a truly genuine person. He was completely himself in all situations and never assimilated to the crowd. I only know of a handful of people with this quality and I have admired them all because it is a flaw that I constantly struggle with myself. His individuality was an inspiration to me.

Secondly, he was a source of encouragement in my life. I am very young and inexperienced in the work field and he was wise beyond his years. He and I had a chance to talk about a job opportunity that I felt very unqualified for. He encouraged me to strive beyond my reach in order to achieve my dreams. He kept repeating "just go for it, what do you have to lose?" Regardless of whether or not I get the job, I owe him a debt for the lessons I learned in the attempt.

The biggest way he touched my life is actually indirectly through my sister, Elizabeth. He was her favorite teacher and mentor. It was through her that I got to know him. She always spoke so highly of him that I had to introduce myself to him. He meant a lot to both she and I and we will remember him fondly for the rest of our lives.

• • •

I wrote this poem on Monday, after I found out what had happened, and I wanted you to have it.

I'm sorry for your loss and for the world's loss. Mr. Cohen was a great guy and a great teacher. I feel very honored having been one of his students.

Today is not a day to cry
and not a day to mourn
But it is a day to remember
the one that we have loved.
Remember him, not in tears

But in secret smiles,
Remember what you did together
all the good and the bad
and you will see he is not lost forever
But forever be in your hearts.

• • •

Before writing this letter, I could not stop
thinking how I could begin it. I was fright-
ened that I would say something that would
trigger anger or sadness. From the bottom of
my heart, I am eternally sorry for the unexpected death of your son. I really do not know
how that sounds coming from somebody
you have never seen or met. For whatever it's
worth I was one of the students that was in
his first AP European History class. Also,
it is an honor to say that I was one of the
students who was close to him. Like everybody else, I cannot believe he is gone. Well…
I just wanted to let you know that he meant
something to me. To me, Mr. Cohen was a
genius and nothing less. He has been the only
teacher that inspired me to study harder and
to do extremely well. For that, I am eternally
grateful. Since I can no longer tell him that in
person, I feel a great need to tell his family. In
our school, it is very uncommon for a teacher
to have that effect on their students. Mr.
Cohen had that effect.

Ever since I met him, I admired him. I

wanted to impress him in some way. I think I never did. Every essay I wrote and every comment I thought out, I took it upon myself to think it thoroughly. I needed to prove myself worthy so that at least for one minute he would think of me as a respectful student.

Mr. Cohen had that exquisite effect on various students. I just wanted to let you know what he did that will influence my life, of course, in a good way, in times to come.

Showing Mr. Cohen my immense gratitude was something I wanted to do. For being one of those teachers that are also your friends. Those you like to talk to and laugh with. As I said, I had to tell you what he meant to me now that I cannot tell him. An inspiration to long for knowledge and learn anything there is to learn.

I apologize for any uneasy aftermath of this letter. Once again, I am eternally sorry.

Wondrous

Some wonder why,
some just wonder
Tonight you might cry
Wondrous?

Tonight I wonder
I just may

that for at least one more day
wonder why they could not stay.

Weep and cry,
tonight I just might try
Life: a puddle...
Maybe so deep or even so dry.

One more day,
would it make a difference?
Some might say nay,
but that I wonder day by day.

One does lament.
It's just a slow descent
In a life that always meant
Do you lament?

Tonight I wonder why
on how tomorrow I just might die.
Tonight I may
wonder what there is to say

To all those souls that cannot stay,
you wondrous people that passed away
may you rest in peace, wonder, and cast away.

• • •

I was a student of your son and brother. On
my behalf I would like to send my condolence. I have had Mr. Cohen for a teacher
for the last two years of history. And I have
enjoyed every minute of those classes. He

taught me a lot and showed me to appreciate history and learn to love it. I hope to have a career in History.

He made the class fun and enjoyable as opposed to stuffy and depressing like my other teacher. He was a cool teacher although his style was very unique, and that also goes for his fashion sense. I am sorry to say that he will no longer be in the class exchanging insults with each other, which was actually a high point on certain days. I am sorry that I will not see the bright and odd assortment of shirts that he chose to wear or his ugly cow-boy boots. He will be missed sorely especially those days, which are dull and gray, which he always managed to brighten up.

When the class would sometimes ask about him, his family, he would answer with pride in his voice. He told us that when he was younger that he would bother his sister with her boyfriends and pull stupid pranks. He told us about breaking into his teacher's office to hand in papers. He told us about his father who was a writer. He also told us that he was writing a book.

I hope this letter brings you some comfort. I don't know what to say and if this letter is all right. I have never lost a teacher, this way. I have lost a friend and I can only imagine the grief of losing a loved one. Good luck.

And I hope this letter is respectful and not inadequate.

• • •

It is very hard to lose a very dear family member, so I can imagine how painful it must be to lose a son. He was my Civics teacher, but he did not only give me knowledge, he also taught me how to work hard and never give up. I am really proud to say I had the great honor of meeting your son. I knew him very little, but ever since I met him I knew he was special.

Mr. Cohen was a very energetic person. He loved dogs and teaching. His life was cut short and although we cannot understand it, we must learn to accept it. All I can tell you is that he is with God, looking down on you and no matter where you go, he'll always be with you. Know that one day you will all be together again.

I know that I can say nothing, or very little to lessen your pain. I thank God that Mr. Cohen came to Nicaragua. This gave me the chance to meet him, to see him every day, learn some of what he knew, and some of what he felt.

Mr. Cohen was full of life and charisma. Everyone who knew him will cherish the

moments they spent with him. I am really
sorry for your loss. His death deprived the
world of his energy and knowledge. He will
be missed. Mr. Cohen is now resting; may he
rest in peace.

• • •

I really don't know how to start this letter, so
I'm just going to go with what I'm feeling.
I feel really sad and I feel really sorry that
this happened. Mr. Cohen was definitely one
of my favorite teachers. I loved his class, it
was honestly the only class that could keep
me awake. It is not his class that I'm gonna
miss; it's Mr. Cohen. I had gotten used to
giving him jokes every time I met him in the
hallway and I had gotten used to his cowboy
boots and his funny walk. I know I'm gonna
miss his face and the sound of him walking
down the hallway. I'm angry at how unfair
everything is. He was so young, he was writing a book, he was very smart; he had plans.
Today is Thursday and I still can't believe
he's gone. It all feels unreal. I feel really bad
and I was just one of his students. I cannot
even begin to imagine what you guys must
feel like. I bet he was a wonderful son. When
we found out the news, many of his students
were crying, so I know he will be missed by
his school, his family, and his friends. We all
loved him a lot.

• • •

When I first heard the news that Mr. Cohen
had left us I was in shock. Mr. Cohen was
my US History teacher this year. He was an
excellent teacher. It amazed me how when
you'd ask him what happened on a certain
date he would know exactly what happened.
I can't believe he's gone. I was just starting to
get used to the noise his boots used to make
as he dragged his feet on the floor, or when
he flicked his keys in the air, or when he was
always with his little computer. It scares me
to think that this could happen to anyone. I'm
really sorry for your loss because it was also a
huge loss to us. I want you to know that Mr.
Cohen was a good man and that you should
have the honor to call him your son, brother,
and friend. Always remember that you are not
alone and don't be afraid to remember him
because memories are what keep our lost ones
alive.

• • •

As one of Mr. Cohen's AP US History students, I am very sorry for your loss. I cannot
imagine what you are going through, but
I still thought you might appreciate a few
words about him from one of his students.

I tend to lean toward the sciences, and I am

planning to study engineering. Last year
I signed up in Mr. Cohen's history class,
because I had to take US History, and I knew
that he was the best qualified teacher for the
class. I did not know him personally then,
but I certainly knew who he was, for he was
not the kind of person that walks around
unnoticed. I admired his uniqueness, for he
seemed to know exactly who he was, and was
not afraid to show it. I had been a student in
an AP History course before, but despite my
good grades, I dropped out of the course at
half year. The teacher was great, but I didn't
find the class stimulating or interesting. After
all, if it's only about memorizing the facts,
just about anyone can learn history by reading
a book. This year I decided to try again, this
time in US and not European history.

I had planned to enroll in AP Physics as well,
until I learned that it was held at the same
time as AP US History. However, I decided
to go to a couple of classes and see what the
teacher was like. I went to the first class,
and I could not believe it! For the first time
I actually laughed (and hard) in a history
lecture! Laugh you say, in a history class? Yes!
Laugh. I was thrilled, and, as always, I went
home and told my Dad all about it. I knew I
would take this class in college, but not with
this teacher. Mr. Cohen analyzed the 'whys'
and 'wherefores,' and did not spend the class
time listing endless dates and names (that

was the book's job). He had a way of keeping to himself, but I immediately realized he was a brilliant person. There were some topics I couldn't wait to hear his opinions about.

Mr. Cohen was definitely a tough grader, and I admit I am a very competitive student. Once, while we were discussing his grading policy and he joked on how 100's are practically nonexistent in history gradebooks, I asked him whether it was actually possible to get a perfect grade on one of his tests. He said it had never happened before, so I challenged him to a little bet: I would surprise him with a one hundred before the end of the year. I always keep my promises, and I had promised myself I would win the bet and make him proud. In his memory, I will still do it, I will score a 5 on the AP and work harder in his honor.

I keep remembering all that he said, the distinct way in which he spoke and even moved, the way he looked at me as if I was going crazy during my usual laughing fits, and I can't help but smile. One thing is certain, I will never forget that cheerful reply he gave me whenever I asked him for college advice: "Go to Wesleyan!"

If this anecdote has even made you smile, then I have fulfilled my purpose. With faith, we can believe Mr. Cohen is watching down on us right now. I think he would want his family to hold on to that faith and live life, giving it a little extra push in his honor.

• • •

I congratulate you for having raised such a fine human being. To me Steve was not only a teacher. He was more. He was my friend. Steve was someone who not only taught me about history, he also taught me about life. If there is one thing that I can assure you it is that his memory will not be forgotten. I only hope there were words to ease the pain you are experiencing in this difficult moment. My deepest regrets.

• • •

Mr. Cohen gave me exactly 77.8, which decreased my average a lot. Sometimes, I stay up all night working on his homework; but all he gave me was B or C. Who would like a teacher like this? Well, I do. He was, is, and will be one of my greatest teachers. He tried to teach us everything he knows. He wanted us to learn everything he knows. He was not a kind of teacher who just gives grades for nothing. After listening to his classes, I decided to be a teacher like him. I am glad that I was able to learn a lot of lessons in his class but regret that it was only a short time.

His time to leave this world had come. When I heard it, it was hard to accept. I still feel like he will come into the class and start the class early in the morning. Even though I am not able to see him anymore, he will be always in my heart. Thank you for reading this letter.

• • •

I was a student of Mr. Cohen's both last year and this year. I am writing you now to tell you that, though I cannot compare my loss to yours, I share your grief.

I was a new student last year and Mr. Cohen was the first teacher I met on my first day. From that very first day, I loved his class and looked forward to it. I had never enjoyed history before last year, but Mr. Cohen knew it so well that he made it seem so real. And his class wasn't a history class where I just memorized facts about <u>what</u> and <u>when</u> we studied, but he taught me <u>how</u> and <u>why</u> the concepts and ideas behind the movements in history. I didn't just learn in his class, I was <u>educated</u> in that he made me, and all his students, understand for ourselves and he challenged us to really think.

But Steve Cohen was more to me than just my teacher. He was my mentor in that I sought his approval in my work and I held his opinion so highly. Today I received my report card and his teacher comment to me was that I had "exceeded class and teacher expectations." That is the best compliment I have <u>ever</u> received. I so greatly respected and admired him. He was a brilliant man and a great teacher, and though I learned so much from him, I know he had much more to teach me. He had a profound impact on me personally and I will carry the knowledge and understanding that I gained through him for the rest of my life. He had been my favorite teacher for over a year, and I think he knew that, other teachers had told him I'd said so. But I knew before and know more clearly now, that he was the best teacher I have ever had. I wish he'd known that too.

It is impossible to understand what has happened. But I want to thank you so much for sharing your son and your brother with us, with me, so that he could teach me and change me as he has. Know I will miss him tremendously.

• • •

FROM A FELLOW TEACHER

Please excuse these torn pages. I have been utterly incapable of writing to you about Steve, and it is only now, in the middle of the night, that I awaken and find it is time.

I have found myself, after my first period class, stalling, shuffling papers around my desk, one eye attuned to the far corner of my window. With a leaden feeling I come to wonder what it is I'm waiting for. In my deepest heart, I still expect Steve to amble around the corner in his curious way.

Steve had such a luminous spirit. It emanated from his eyes, particularly. I think he knew the intensity of his look, for there were times when he almost seemed to shield us from it, lowering his head as if to lessen the impact of his gaze. He could, and did, question almost anything, especially his friends.

My own pain is mainly one of stunted promise. Your own, composed of a fuller picture of all Steve was and was going to be, is overwhelming. I cannot express my condolences adequately, but I wish you to know that you and your family are in my thoughts, as is Steve.

I am so glad we were able to meet. Everyone's grief has taken so many forms. I hope the image of us as Steve's friends had a positive side, as did yours as his family for us.

PART SEVEN
Jesus In Singapore

Frustrated and unable to come up with a solution Saren desires the help of his mother. Seeking her out in the Ocean he becomes the first to cross over into the Sea, although those who try to follow are dissolved by the salt of the water.

—*The History of Lathrim*

Chapter One

The year after Stephen died I took to traveling like a vagabond to escape my grief, as if that were even possible.

Stephen went everywhere with me, coexistent in every waking thought and in my dreams as well. "I'll be looking at the moon/But I'll be seeing you," as in the wistful lyrics from a pre-war love song. I had to visit Singapore with my brother during July to inspect a large boat hoist, a machine able to pick a 500-ton boat out of the water and dry dock it on land. Our business was repairing fishing boats in a shipyard. This large machine had come on the market, unexpectedly, and we wanted to consider it while the opportunity existed. I was in Switzerland on one of my journeys. My brother faxed the information to me, and we booked separate flights.

Singapore is not part of the world one visits for a long weekend, the flight a strenuous 30 hours of constant travel, arriving finally on the other side of the world at two in the morning. There was a squash court in the hotel. I brought my racquet and hit the ball around before lunch to clear the cobwebs. Physically exhausted, yet far from calm, I turned on the television and lay back on my bed, in this monastic cell of a modern hotel. It was a hollowed out core/atrium lobby with room-pods on the periphery and a balcony, before which stretched the blatantly modern city of Singapore with its high-rise downtown of commercial buildings, like Miami Beach.

"Who was Jesus?" The theme of an afternoon talk show on ABC, which I chanced to tune in, moderated by Hugh Downs. He was bemused by the passion of his four guests, whom I shall try to describe from memory. I could request the transcript of the show if I really wanted to be accurate, but I would rather let my own faulty recollection and bias guide the purpose of my story.

There were four panelists, names unimportant for the moment, but their demeanor remains reasonably clear. A Catholic priest spoke with deep and regretful apology to the rabbi for all the misdeeds of the Church during its millennium of persecution. "But we are still the one true faith and all others are delusions," he said. I loved his patronizing smile at the rabbi, an ultra-Orthodox Jew from Brooklyn, scarcely representative of contemporary Jewish thought, but a scholar of religious texts, who probably knew his Gospel better than the three Christians.

"Jesus was a historical figure," he insisted. "Anti-Semitism has existed from the very beginning of Christianity. You can't just apologize. You have to change at the very roots."

The priest smiled as if a good confession had absolved everything. They had a lively debate about Jesus who came to earth to reassure mankind that victory was possible, that suffering had a goal. "Not so," said the rabbi. "At best, Jesus may have been God's instrument for making the morality of the Torah known to people everywhere."

The Baptist insisted we had to believe in the whole package in order to be saved from eternal damnation—Jesus, Son of the Living God, Redeemer of Mankind, Resurrection. No other option available. I wondered where that left the Buddhists, Muslims, and Hindus. The ultra-Orthodox became more paranoid. For all we knew, I thought, Jesus might have come and gone many times, without anyone realizing it, doing good in small ways that went unnoticed, for wasn't it important not to take credit for charity? Isn't there a little bit of the divine in everyone, we of cosmic dust incarnate, each of us with some capability to transform that divine spark into real deeds of valor?

As for the last member of the panel, she truly dwelt out in the ether. An Evangelist, she was committed to bringing the good news that faith in Jesus will save us. "Just give me Jesus," she declared. "He is relevant in our daily life." She raised her eyes to heaven like an itinerant preacher. "God's beloved Son walked on water. He gave his life as ransom for the many." My beloved son could not even swim, let alone walk on water. And he gave his life to save a drowning dog.

To digress, let me explain what happened in Geneva, Switzerland, where my wife and I had been just two weeks before Singapore. Serene and beautiful Geneva on Lac Léman marks the source of the Rhône as it rushes through the center of the city and into France and the Mediterranean. Geneva opens one's senses in quite an unexpected way. It is what I love about travel.

In the old city, a festival of music had just begun, the variety staggering: ancient and ethnic, baroque, opera, blues, reggae, Latino, and, of course, rock and roll. People were dispersed in so many different locations during the day and evening that it never seemed crowded, with seating always available. Music, by acclaim, the universal language. The logo on programs and posters all had the hieroglyphics of musical notation—note signs, brackets, and an occasional little heart shape signifying, no doubt, love. How happy everyone seemed!

We had spit-roasted chicken in a restaurant in the old square and discovered we were in the epicenter of the festival. We found our way through streets to the Saint-Pierre Cathedral, where people gathered at twilight for an organ concert. We entered a chapel in the cathedral, glowing with light and already filled, and sat in the next-to-last row, as kindly folk tucked themselves along the pew to accommodate two more bottoms. In the mid-panel of stained glass, an image of Christ stared piercingly down at us and, I thought, with his red hair and beard, he resembled Stephen.

I promptly dozed off, lulled by that soothing Bach on the organ, chin in hand, elbow balanced precariously on my knee and fell, for just a millisecond, asleep; my elbow slipped, my tinker-toy arm went flop, and I awoke with a start, apologizing to my neighbors next to me and in the row behind.

"You were snoring," my wife said.

That night when we returned to our comfortable room in the Hotel des Bergues, on the opposite side of the old town, at the beginning of the spillway into the Rhône, I had a dream.

I dreamed I was sitting in a parked car on a shady street with the driver's door open. A puppy, out on his walk with a young man, came trotting down the sidewalk towards me. Seeing my open door, he ran to the car and jumped into my lap and licked my face, desperate for affection. It was, I think, a Chinese Shar-Pei, with unusual short hair and wrinkled skin like a human body, a puppy, a baby Stephen. It promptly peed in my lap. His owner apologized for the wet spot and picked the dog up. I replied, *It's all right*, too overjoyed with my brief visit to complain and marveling how Steve had visited me in this form. For it truly seemed that Steve was trying to communicate to me his love in the form of this cuddly, infant dog.

Why a dog? I wondered upon awakening. Not a hopeful sign in the Hindu cycles of reincarnation, returned to me as the symbol of his demise, sacrificed for an animal. How many years and cycles would I have to wait for his real form to appear? And he had the idea backwards. Didn't we usually sacrifice animals to placate some God? Stephen, now Lord of Dogs. Surely that warm, cuddly being, kissing my face, had been the Stephen of his infancy as I used to hold him tenderly in my arms and felt his diaper grow damp, as he had so often peed, loved and contented, on my lap. I had to be content with his return, in whatever form it took.

Johann Sebastian Bach had a genius for combining both joy and grief in his music. Stephen drowned on the 17th of October, 1999. My wife, who was his stepmother, and I had attended a Sunday concert of Bach's Goldberg Variations for harpsichord at a nearby church. The soloist performed brilliantly, a requiem for Stephen, as it developed. Earlier that day he had drowned, thousands of miles away in the Pacific Ocean. My brilliant, sweet son gone from our life. Could I ever enjoy divine Bach again?

How Stephen, who was adopted, loved music! He had cartons of CDs, hundreds of them, but mostly classic rock from the 70s. He left them in our cellar when he went to Nicaragua, a small fortune in CDs, which I sorted out to give his sister. I attributed his love of music to his birth family, a grandparent, head of the music department of a well-known university.

My tale of two cities, Singapore and Geneva, becomes

even more mysterious. We went, my wife and I, to a museum containing early 20th-century paintings in a 19th-century mansion, a neighborhood of similarly gracious buildings. As we strolled through small rooms, we heard a baroque piece in rehearsal which, time and again, the players worked hard at getting just right. When we came to their room, we found a trio—an oboist, a violinist, and a pianist. Chairs had been set up in the gallery for a concert at two in the afternoon. A young woman, the oboe player, seemed quite distressed as if their playing, to our ears sublime, could not find the precise sound she required. It was a labor in which they all seemed oddly distressed, a labor of love which later would give birth to a vision of Stephen.

"Is that by Corelli?" I asked, during a pause.

"It's Bach's Oboe Concerto," she replied.

"Will you be playing here?"

"At La Chapelle de l'Oratoire on Rue-Tabazan," she said. "You don't need tickets, just come. All the concerts are free."

The players were young, the oboist slender and unusually pretty. She played her instrument with intensity, challenging the others with her passion. It seemed more than just a rehearsal difficulty. As we left the museum looking at our street map, a man offered assistance, an American who traveled often to Geneva. He found our location on the map quickly. We explained about a group rehearsing inside, wanting to attend their concert.

"That's my daughter," he replied.

"Is there some problem?" I asked.

"Two of their group, a violin and cello, have not arrived yet. She's quite upset."

My son returned to me in another dream, not as a dog this time, but in his own form. His stepmother, Sylvia, and I met him in a park where he was walking with a girlfriend. It was summer and they dressed casually. She was slender and attractive, in the way he liked, with long brown hair and pretty features. Not surprisingly, she looked like the oboe player. They were holding hands, and I could see he was very happy. I knew Stephen would devote himself to one woman, and I was pleased he had found her, at last.

"Your son wears interesting clothes," she commented. He had on one of his bright Hawaiian shirts, his trademark plumage. She wore a modest blouse, belted at the waist, her skirt of such diaphanous cloth it shimmered in the breeze.

The Stephen in my dream, as in life, was just over six feet tall. I would say, with a father's pride, that my son was handsome. Stephen had auburn hair and when he let it grow, a red beard, although he was clean shaven in my dream. He walked with an awkward shuffle because his feet toed in. He usually wore cowboy boots with heels trashed by the angle of his gait. We had the same shoe size, and I often lent him sneakers or a pair of loafers for dress-up if he had come to visit without enough to wear.

Sylvia took his new friend, arm-in-arm, for a walk to tell her about Steve, while he and I continued on along the sandy path under swaying green boughs.

"I'm worried Dad," he said. "How do I explain when I have to leave? You know, when I have to go back to heaven."

"It will be like a business trip," I replied.

"I'll always return, but how will I explain my absence?"

"She'll understand," I counseled. "Don't worry."

It made me happy to think I had conjured for him the

loving relationship he so wanted. If I could just visit with him more often, even in dreams, I knew my own grief would subside. But grief is an illness from which we can never fully recover or be inoculated against. Sooner or later it infects everyone. And isn't that what this story is about? How to endure grief when someone we love dies suddenly?

The festival continued on the Acropolis in Geneva. Restaurants were crowded at lunch, overflowing onto sidewalk tables. How happy everyone looked with plenty of food to eat and free music. We walked from the square past antique shops and outdoor stalls selling ethnic fast food—humus and shish kebab, falafel with yogurt wrapped in flatbread. Crowds had gathered before a tented stage where musicians from Senegal in long, red robes, beat rhythm with drumsticks and bongos. A tall blond lady danced in the crowd, her whirling arms and hips keeping time. We rounded a corner, found Rue Tabazan, and continued until we reached a small church. In the rear courtyard the young lady, Ariana, was rehearsing. Her father stood under a tree watching. He smiled, recognizing us.

Ariana entered through a rear door with her two accompanists. I believe that was her name, or if not, it belongs here in my story with its three alephs in its spelling as if to constitute a new beginning, an alpha to Stephen's omega. Appropriate, also, that Bach's Oboe Concerto was the divine medium of his return, as Bach's Goldberg Variations had been when he died. Lovely Ariana looked around, one last time, hoping her missing players were somewhere in the crowd. She gathered her violinist and pianist and began to play Bach. She was determined to evoke the sweet sadness of the music, exalted, tragic and hopeful, in one continuous line. She scarcely took a breath.

The chapel was spare and elegant, two steps up from the

congregation to the platform where they were playing, double columns on either side supporting a second level. It had been a Protestant church once, no decoration save for a bare timber cross about ten feet tall by six.

I felt Stephen enter me then, filling my body with such pure love and emotion that I could scarcely believe or understand how two of us could fill one space.

Before my brother arrived in Singapore, I resolved to visit some temples and say a prayer for Stephen in each one. When I walked out of the air-conditioned lobby into the July humidity of the equator, it was difficult to breathe. Although I had intended to walk, I saw taxicabs in front of the hotel and decided to take the doorman's offer to call one over.

"Where would you like to go?" Most Singaporeans spoke English. I told him my son had died recently, and I wanted to pray for him in the various faiths of Singapore: Chinese, Hindu, and Muslim. I was hedging all my bets, I explained. The Chinese love to gamble, and he laughed.

"I will take you," he said, "and we will pray together. My mother died not long ago." I was glad to have a guide, for I would never have found the temples without him.

We parked in front of a small shrine on a narrow street— temple of the "Fat Buddha," my guide announced. We entered through an open arch, and he explained what I needed to do. "The Chinese are not fussy about religion," he explained. "If you have a good heart, that's enough."

I purchased incense sticks which he lit for us both. We placed clusters of three in sand-filled urns, which held guttering candles other petitioners had put there, curling sweet incense into the air. In the alcove off the street sat a large

241

Buddha. After we made our offering, he stood in front of Buddha and said, "Now pray for whatever you like, for prosperity, good health."

I asked for Buddha's blessing on my son. A sense of holiness pervaded this sanctuary where people could visit as the spirit moved them.

We drove just around the corner and arrived at the Hindu temple, a famous shrine with images of gods on its roof and all around its courtyard, modeled in boldly-glazed colors, life-sized terracotta statues, both human as well as animal, a colorful museum full of vibrant paintings and sculpture.

"You pay to make your offering and take photographs." He guided me to a sari-clad woman, and I gave her my five Singapore dollars to enter the temple. He did likewise and led me to the center shrine where he bowed his head. I stood next to him and did the same, all lines of communication open, I hoped, for there were many ways to access the Holy Spirit in this Hindu temple. I prayed a blessing for Stephen.

Another Chinese temple stood across from a park against a background of modern buildings, surrounded by a wrought iron fence painted bright red. Inside, a monk prayed with a family before a small shrine, banging a drum three times and ringing a sweet tinkling bell. We lit wax candles, placing each one in a pot filled with sand on either side of the main shrine. In the middle three urns, we put incense sticks, three each, which we had lit in the candle flame. We said our prayers and then, for good luck, purchased stacks of tissue paper, symbolizing money, printed in red and gold with the images of three wise men, called Fu Lu Soh: longevity, prosperity, and good luck. Nearby, we joined several people and tossed our money into an oven, where ashes glowed orange and the heat singed the hair on one's wrist.

"The Chinese believe if you make an offering to Buddha, he will return it back to you many times over." My driver smiled. "The more you pray," he said, "the better you will feel."

My driver parked in front of a nearby mosque. "The stairs go up to a very holy place." He pointed out his window. "I can't go in there."

I entered the main sanctuary feeling less sure of myself without a guide. Arab traders, long ago, plied the South China Sea and spread the word of Allah. Early afternoon, three men inside glanced indifferently at me. I retreated, not wanting to offend, and mounted steps to the shrine on the top. I said my brief Stephen prayer to Muhammad, to Moses, and to Confucius, to all the holy people, known and unknown in every land who had graced this holy world of the animate and sentient. Reverence for all religion and for all life is what I felt then. And I gave thanks. And, as my driver predicted, I felt better.

One last prayer at a very old Chinese temple that developers were planning to relocate. The property had grown too valuable. This time a priestess prayed for me. "What is your name?" she asked. I gave her Stephen's name. It was for him the bell tolled and the drum banged, for my son. It was beautiful inside with many icons painted brightly and hanging coils of incense.

My guide was doing some serious praying on his own before a fierce warrior, and I waited for him near the entrance, guarded by stone lions. He threw two pieces of wood in the air. They fell to the ground with a clattering sound. They were dice, I realized. He completed several more tosses, letting them fall randomly on the floor, inspecting the result.

"I asked Buddha for help," he explained. "The first time, one dice up, one down. Buddha says okay to ask a favor. I throw a second time, both dice up. Buddha angry. I throw again, one up, one down. Buddha says okay to make a wish. Today is the lottery, so I ask Buddha for a lucky number. I have to buy a new cab, and they are very expensive. I throw the dice again to get a number—8902." On the way back to the hotel, we drove to the Government Lottery Office.

"Is it all right if I bet on the same number?" I asked.

"Not a problem," he replied. "If we win, I'll call you at your hotel tonight." I gave him $10 to buy me two tickets. As we drove back to the hotel, my eloquent guide through the ecumenical Singapore world said, "I will carry your son with me in my heart. He is sitting next to you, always, like my mother sits next to me. Your son will look out for you." I never heard from the driver again.

And that ends my story, with a lottery bet and a cab driver.

When I returned to the United States, I had another dream. Stephen and I were walking with our arms interlocked like dear friends. We came to a street intersection, and he took my hand, as if I were the child, as I did for him when we crossed the street. It gave me great comfort to be in his firm grip. We continued through the park that seemed to be in all my dreams of Steve, and although we did not speak to one another, I knew we were both very happy.

Chapter Two

I search for Stephen through layers of memory, visited by him from a different world of dream. Steve and I are traveling in two parallel universes, and he reaches across to pull me into his world. Dreams are like a cosmic gravity across these parallel worlds, full of the intense attraction of our love for one another, and I am happy to be reunited with him.

"Have you brought any homework with you?" I ask in one early dream.

"Not this time," he replies.

They were walking along a hill overlooking the Pacific Ocean early Sunday morning—three men, two women, one the owner of a dog, and Stephen amongst them—disappointed their schooner cruise had been cancelled because of the storm. Giant surf from the hurricane that had just swept over Nicaragua smashed the rocky shore below. The dog ran from the group to hunt crabs along the shoreline, where the rocks, slippery with seaweed and green algae, gave no footing even to four scrambling paws. It slipped into the water and was quickly pulled out to sea. The woman looked at Steve imploring—that one fatal look—and he ran down the hill, alarmed at the dog's peril.

"Don't go," his friends yelled. "It's too dangerous."

Stephen reached the bottom of the cliff. The dog was drifting further away. He called to it in a reassuring way. He left his shoes, his wallet, and his car keys in a neat pile. He hated the beach and had probably not gone for a swim during his entire time in Nicaragua. As a child he had been afraid to dive headfirst into a swimming pool.

Stephen waded in the only way possible—a deceptively calm place, a lagoon just inside a natural breakwater of rocks tumbled from the cliff. The waves crashed against the stone splashing 15 feet in the air. Somehow he crossed the barrier, a rugged protection offered by the rocks, crawling through a narrow space between them. Then, once past that safe point, the waves took control. They tumbled him mercilessly back against the granite rock time and again, and then he floated past the breakwater, pulled by the undertow out towards the ocean and the dog who struggled no longer.

Aware now of his own doom, he cried out, "Help me!" conscious for only a few moments more. Then he sank, a half-submerged torso, face down, cresting each rolling wave.

One friend reached the lagoon and wisely turned back. The other, a strong swimmer, tried to scale the blitz of wave on rock. He understood better than Steve how to tread water and not fight the undertow, to wait patiently until one could swim, angling towards the beach that lay just a few hundred yards south. But he couldn't get through, tossed back into the lagoon, torn and bruised.

Gagging for air, what terror did Stephen perceive before he mercifully lost consciousness? How does the body drown? Not like the dream-time passing of the elderly, peaceful and anesthetized by sleep.

Stephen's friends found two men fishing along the beach. One of them rowed a skiff out and pushed him closer to the beach, where the other threw out his long lead-weighted line and hook, which *they attached to his underwear and pulled him in—fisher of Steve's body as I am fisher of Steve's soul.*

What is it about dreams that make us ponder them with such apprehension and joy? We are never more creative than dreaming our own scenario, interacting with characters— people once loved or feared—in a play that seems chosen to entertain, enlighten, and yet leave us with even more vexing questions.

I wonder now if there might be a life after. Why has my son's energy survived in thoughts and images and feelings all combined? My mind scans like a short-wave antenna for a signal in the noise and my son is received. He comes in to my dream life loud and clear, more vivid than in real life, and we interact in ways I could never have imagined nor predicted. We have bridged the gap and are together again in a sacred way that I treasure because I still know deep in my heart he has died.

Stephen's voice on his Mac computer is my constant reminder. "I'll be back," he predicted, the timbre of his voice so recognizable even through the cheap speaker. "I'll be back," not to haunt you but to bring you joy.

One month after he drowned, I dream of having a conversation with Steve in a darkened room. His voice sounds otherworldly like a 45 RPM record running at 33 RPM. He is reflective, even sad, regarding his romantic aspirations and his attempts to find a true mate, a woman to settle down with and raise children. Every so often I catch a glimpse of his close-trimmed red beard, as if a rotating lighthouse beacon crosses his face while he stands near me, illuminating him for a brief moment.

"Yeah, Dad, well I'm still trying," he concludes. "I guess I should give her a call."

"Who is she?" I ask. He pauses as if perplexed by my question, not able to provide an answer.

Another night, he is standing next to me as we record our conversation together on a small palm-held recorder. I am going to tell his story—the story of Stephen, the great questioner—who wanted to know WHY? In this dream his figure is clearer but his features are indistinct. His voice is as expressive as a radio announcer, an actor, a teacher.

In December, two months after he died, I dream of Stephen walking down the street where I lived as a child for almost 15 years. He is with James, one of his college friends. They are in front of our next door neighbor's house. Steve looks across the street to where I am standing partially hidden by a maple tree.

"What, Dad?" he questions.

Do you need a ride anywhere? I want to ask. I hide behind the tree and make no response, watching him, knowing he has died. I can't take him anywhere, anymore, but, oddly, I think he believes he is still with the living.

And the first dream of the millennium, in January, I am standing in an empty apartment. A small dog and two ferrets are there with me. I go to leave and feel the dog grab me around the ankle with its front paws, whining for me to stay. I reach down and pick it up, cradling him in my arms. The dog kisses me and nuzzles my chin with its snub nose. Its hair is silky and auburn colored like Steve. Licking my face, the animal expresses a love for me with exquisite charm. I feel my chest swell with love and tenderness, in turn, realizing that this dog is Stephen transformed, trying to hug my face between its two small, outstretched paws, as I used to snuggle him as a child. I am ineffably happy to meet him again, even as a dog, as

248

the reincarnation, perhaps, of the dog he tried to save.

I have come to the edge of land in the first of three dreams early in 2001. Waves, in concentric, even crests, are crashing upon the shore. They appear safe and tempt me to body surf. As a wave recedes I walk quickly over damp sand into the water, submerging beneath a wave. In the ebb and pull beneath the surface, the wave flows over me, and I feel someone's hands underneath as if to raise me back up to the calm space between the cresting waves. I wonder, in my dream, if Stephen is helping me, but I am not in danger, yet, nor in need of being rescued.

A month later I attend a service to honor the anniversary of my sister's death. Each time I enter a holy place it is time to grieve for my son as well. On the way home, I sob out loud, "Stephen, I miss you," venting the emotion I must discreetly conceal in church. No one hears me on a cold March street, the trees bare, my windows rolled up tight. "Please visit me more often in my dreams," I beg Stephen. And that night my wish is granted.

It is a dream like all my favorite dreams of Steve; we are walking through a park conversing, wonderfully, about a subject that eludes my comprehension except for the repeated use of a word in an illogical context. The word is "shake." I don't have a clue what he means.

"What is that word you are using?" I ask.

We reach the edge of land, standing on a low cliff overlooking the ocean.

"Shake?" he repeats. "Oh, 'shake' is a word we use over there." He gestures out over the water into a darkening cosmic space.

I am immensely happy at this revelation, brimming with such innocent joy in his presence. My dream is almost a cure for the grief of my day.

In the spring of that year I have a playful dream-visit in which Stephen shows me his newly acquired skill, an ability to make himself invisible and to reappear whenever he wants. We are standing at the end of a long line, rising up the concrete steps of a stadium. I think it is to buy concert tickets. I am anxious about the delay. Steve suddenly becomes transparent. I see his outline form but to everyone else he is invisible. He reappears further up the line. People express mild surprise that he is in front of them, but as they didn't see him arrive or butt in, they merely assume he has been there all along.

Steve enjoys the trick he plays, moving quickly up the long gray stadium steps reaching into the sky, enjoying my astonishment way back at the bottom of the line. He shrugs his shoulders with a look of joy at his new skill, reappearing each time without any objection from the people he has stepped slyly in front of. He looks at me now as if to say, "Don't worry; see how easily I am able to get along." He has figured out how to get to the head of the line, a talent I admire. I realize he is speedily traversing a long line into heaven, where he disappears from my view.

PART EIGHT
Letting Go

Saren never seems to grow older, even as the years passed. Troubled by the limits of his own understanding, and why Ezmath wants these wonderful rushes of creativity to be dampened, he develops a method by which everyone might mentally put themselves in tune with one another to such a degree that they could share thoughts. The closer in tune they become the longer this sharing would last. And, as long as each member of the group shares thoughts periodically with at least one other, nothing would ever be lost from the group consciousness.

—*The History of Lathrim*

Chapter One

On the train to New York two years later I sat next to a young man who, with his auburn hair and friendly smile, reminded me of Stephen. He nodded hello, then went back to watching a James Bond movie on his laptop. Most of the seats were taken. My wife sat across the aisle from me next to a young woman, also traveling alone.

We were going to visit our son's friend, who had shared a senior year dorm with Stephen and his dog. Now she had Kinneson all to herself, a 13-year-old mix of Newfoundland, German shepherd, and husky, which could explain his howling-speak in dog tongue. He was a large black dog with tan legs. Elisabeth had rescued Kinneson from Nicaragua a year after Stephen's death.

When my neighbor's movie ended, we began to chat. He was an architect living in Boston, visiting his fiancée in New York City. Separate careers made the weekend commute necessary until they resolved the geography of their love. He had majored in the liberal arts and did graduate work at Cornell.

"My son was accepted at Cornell," I told him. "We drove out one weekend to inspect the school, took a quick walk around campus, got back in the car, and drove home. 'I don't want to go there,' Steve said. 'They have a reputation for working too hard.' He went to Wesleyan, instead."

"He was right about that," the young man replied. "What's your son doing now?"

"He went to graduate school and wound up teaching history in Nicaragua, where he accidentally drowned."

"Oh, I'm sorry," the architect said. My wife didn't like me to mention Stephen to anyone, especially strangers. *It's not fair to them* she'd say. But it was one of my ways of keeping him alive. The architect had a strong foundation. He could handle a sad story.

"We're going to visit my son's dog. We haven't seen him since just before Steve died. Two years now. I wonder if he'll remember me."

"Don't worry," he replied. "Dogs never forget."

We pulled into Penn Station. I introduced him to my wife, Sylvia, and we wished one another well. He was a big man. I let him shoulder his bag and exit in front of us. All my wife needed was one look.

"You told him about Steve."

Sheepishly, I nodded *yes*. "He reminded me of him."

"I know," she said, ruefully.

The next morning, we took a cab to 24th and Third Avenue, got out at the corner, and walked slowly towards Elisabeth's apartment, a nondescript high-rise in a quiet neighborhood. Just then, we saw Kinneson pulling Elisabeth along the sidewalk. Sylvia went to meet them as I followed, reluctantly, wondering how to express grief to a dog who loved one's son as much as you did, who was beloved by him?

Kinneson had been kept hidden the entire senior year in the dorm shared with Elisabeth and her cat, and taken out by

Steve, surreptitiously, on his nocturnal strolls. Stephen skipped more classes than he attended, believing his encyclopedic mind would let him fake his way through, and it almost did, just two credits short of graduating. Kinneson, under cover, came before class. Who could resist the friendly dog?

Elisabeth, as beautiful as ever, had a way of making herself modest in her bulky army coat, buttoned at the top, and low military boots, not flattering but very practical. Goodness glowed from her smile. She and Sylvia hugged one another, and I waited my turn.

"Hello, Kinneson...How are you?" sang Sylvia like a song to her aging friend, last seen in Nicaragua. "Oh, it's good to see you."

"Hello, Joel," said Elisabeth. "I'm so glad you came." We had grown closer since Steve died, more like family. We embraced and I felt tears beginning.

Kinneson shuffled over to me, sniffed my proffered hand and stuck his head between my knees as if he were plugging himself into a socket. For a moment he stood still as I quietly rubbed his ears and neck, a moment of silent grief for his lost master...for my son. And then he pulled his head out and looked up at me, and I said, "Hello, Kinneson. How are you?" He didn't howl his husky sound, and he couldn't jump on arthritic hind legs. He was my ghost of Steve, my son's love still inside him, the love of 11 years they shared.

Had loving Kinneson doomed Stephen, who leaped into the Pacific Ocean in a vain attempt to save his friend's dog? It didn't make any difference to Steve, he had to help. I realized that's why I couldn't face Kinneson until now.

What were we going to do with Kinneson that week Stephen died?

"Put him to sleep," I said to his friend George. "Let's assume Stephen is in heaven. Why should we deprive him of his dog?" I was angry at Kinneson for the need he created in Steve's life. I was judge of my son's dog, showing him no mercy.

"You can't do that," George said. "Kinneson means too much to all of us. Elisabeth would be shattered with both gone. We'll figure something out."

Steve's sister, Louise, arranged for one of his teacher friends to take Kinneson. He survived another year, until Elisabeth made her pilgrimage to Nicaragua and brought him back. The teacher was leaving for a job in India and had arranged to leave Kinneson with someone else.

"Do you want to go for a walk?" asked Elisabeth. "Here, you take his leash."

Down the block we went with Kinneson pulling to the end of his long leash. I was amazed how strong he was, even with his hindquarters collapsing beneath him.

"Kinneson was hit by a car and broke his hip, right after Steve first got him."

"I forgot," I replied. "That must have been the five-hundred-dollar emergency sophomore year."

"He's still in good condition," said Elisabeth. "I work just a few blocks away, so I can come back on lunch break and take him for a walk."

I thought of Steve on his long hikes around Providence with Kinneson. Once, my brother and I found them on Atwells Avenue, several miles from Steve's apartment. We trailed him in the car, until Steve chanced to look around, startled, and waved at us. He and Kinneson often wandered the elegant Swan Point Cemetery at night. Sometimes Steve would stop by a tomb, survey the night sky, and smoke a joint in this peaceful place. One night Kinneson chased a muskrat into the river, and as they thrashed about in the water, Steve yelled to him to come back, afraid his dog would drown. Now, what irony: Stephen became the first to use the family plot.

I began to talk softly to Kinneson as we walked. He pulled me wherever he wanted to go. "Good boy, Kinneson." He'd turn around and cock his head. "Do you remember me?" I asked. And off he'd limp again. I was crying pretty steadily now, imagining Stephen walking with us, invisible except for the love that flowed between us.

Elisabeth took my arm and gave me one of her big smiles. She had gotten past grief into a kind of beatitude, thankful for Steve and his generous help in her life, thankful she could repay him by caring for Kinneson.

"I'm much more independent now," she said. "I've learned so much from Steve. I'm finally growing up."

"What a lucky dog, to have you," I said.

"I took Kinneson to the veterinarian when we got back from Nicaragua, and he said Kinneson is in good shape and should live another two years...One to go, if he's lucky."

We turned south on Second Avenue, and Elisabeth pointed towards Bellevue Hospital where they brought the Twin Towers survivors. It had been a season of grief for everyone.

"I wonder what Stephen would have made of all these events?" I asked. "He missed the millennium and another war, big stuff for a historian."

"He's watching," replied Elisabeth. "Don't worry, he knows all about it."

"I bet he's optimistic that life will get better."

Around another block, Elisabeth took the leash back with a better sense of where Kinneson wanted to go, which trees to sniff, and which wire barriers to stumble over, placed to prevent dogs from peeing on the tree.

"You're providing assisted care for Kinneson," my wife said. "He's getting old." It was on her mind. She had taken care of her father in his own home. He died at 95, the same year as Steve.

"Tell me about it," Elisabeth laughed, "all the vets and swim therapy and medicine and food…He eats me out of house and home."

"He's a living memorial," I said.

When we approached another dog on a leash, Elisabeth brought Kinneson back to the safety of her legs. He'd stop, half-squatting, perk his ears inquisitively, as if he forgot he was supposed to growl and tug at the leash. At the sight of Kinneson, the other dogs barked aggressively. Poor Kinneson didn't know what to make of it.

"I have to protect him," said Elisabeth. "He would never hurt a flea."

"I haven't been much help," I said, back in Elisabeth's apartment.

"I understand how you felt," she replied.

"I was angry. Thank God you persisted and took care of him."

"Your daughter was a big help. When Kinneson was attacked by a Rottweiler I knew I had to get him. There's no leash law in Nicaragua." She laughed. "He was a victim of dog terrorism."

Louise had remarked how docile Kinneson had become, following Elisabeth around, keeping her in his sight. Now, he sprawled quite contented at her feet with one of Elisabeth's cats snuggling next to him.

"A case of unrequited love," said Elisabeth. "She's crazy about Kinneson and he doesn't pay her any attention."

Elisabeth's studio apartment had a moderate amount of clutter, not as bad as she had warned. "My place is a mess. There was a good reason Steve and I got along so well," she had warned. How lucky Kinneson was to have Steve's love and now Elisabeth's. He got to his feet with difficulty and limped over to me with a mournful look. I caressed my son's devoted friend, his life cycle complete from puppy to old man, a mystery for me to comprehend. I would have abandoned him. Elisabeth had saved us both.

Oh Kinneson, if you could only tell me about Stephen, whose brief life you shared more than anyone. I'm filled with such longing to know my son and the man he would have become. You spoke to me, Kinneson, when you were young, when I climbed stairs to Steve's apartment in Providence. I could hear you whining behind the door. "Be quiet," Steve urged. "It's only Dad." And you jumped into my arms and licked my face. I always hugged my son, whom you had all to yourself in that alcove under the eaves on Armington Street, with his neatly stacked cases of videos and books and dust everywhere and fur balls.

One year later, on his way to Nicaragua, Steve brought us his boxed-up books and clothes, and left them behind in our cellar with his old Mac computer, unwashed clothes, still redolent of his Steve-odor, my deepest and most primitive memory. Ah, Kinneson, I am like you, a dog in my memory of Steve's smell. Surely you remember me.

Several months after the funeral, Elisabeth took one of Steve's T-shirts so she could preserve her own memory of him. And I gave her the cap he often wore, icon of his college days.

"Why hasn't Steve come to me in my dreams?" I asked Sylvia. "It's been a long while."

"He's very busy right now," she replied, "meeting Socrates, Saint Augustine, and George Washington…all his heroes."

And as if to reassure me that he hadn't forgotten, soon after, I had my hoped-for dream.

I dreamt of Steve as an angel with wings, embracing me in an affectionate flurry of feathers. He had a pony-sized dog with him, Kinneson grown larger. Stephen not only could fly but he could sit on his pony-dog and go for a ride.

Stephen had his dream world, too. It was called "Dungeons and Dragons." I could never understand why he was so fascinated by it. At lunch, while sitting in the Blue Water Grill, a crowded cafe in Union Square, I asked Elisabeth how James and George, his friends, and Stephen could play one game year after year.

"Oh, I played it, too," replied Elisabeth.

The tables outside were filled on this sunny November day and the main dining room was packed, so we sat upstairs in the mezzanine, where a few tables remained.

"How did Stephen's book, *The History of Lathrim*, fit in?" I asked. "The one he was working on for so long."

"It was Steve's world," replied Elisabeth, "evolving over the millennia with gods and humans struggling to coexist." She smiled. "And of course lots of good and evil. Steve envied James' ability to create a narrative off the top of his head, which is what a good dungeon master is supposed to do, send you off on some adventure in the character you choose. James was the best D & D master of our group. He was brilliant!"

"But Steve's story was more a summary of history, a very

tightly written two hundred pages."

"Steve was going to take us through his world, challenging us along the way. We'd fill in the narrative with our own story as we played the game. Steve's history was just a guide. He wrote it down, where James could rattle it off the top of his head."

"What was Steve's favorite character?"

"Oh, Paladin. No doubt about it!" Elisabeth had not hesitated. "He was always on the side of good. You know—protect the innocent, save the fair maiden, rescue the beleaguered."

Jump into the Pacific to save the fair maiden's dog, I thought.

"Was Steve afraid he wouldn't live up to his intelligence?"

"What do you mean?"

"If he tried too hard and still failed."

"Oh no, Steve wasn't into being better than anyone else. He was just Steve, not competitive, not interested in taking credit. Whatever he knew, he shared. He always helped his friends with counsel. He lent us money without ever expecting its return. He knew he could count on your backing him up."

I laughed. "You mean he took from the rich and gave to the poor...like Robin Hood."

"Like a Paladin. Do good for its own sake. That's why we all loved him so much. He was the spoke of the wheel that kept all his friends together. He was an idealist, all right."

"I don't know where he got that from."

"You had an influence on him," she said. "A very big influence."

She had said, finally, what I had wanted to hear.

"It took me until age forty to figure out how to live with the good and evil in my world. That's when I met Sylvia, come to think of it."

Sylvia laughed. "Don't believe that for a minute."

We were almost finished with lunch. The afternoon had worn on, diners had come and gone; outside, on the sidewalk, tables were still full. It was good to feel safe again in New York. It always amazed me how cities could provide almost everyone with sustenance—a glass of wine or a Greek salad, if that's what you wanted.

Our table had grown silent. Elisabeth was sitting in between Sylvia and me, one hand on the table bunched into a fist. I covered it with my own and she unclenched her hand and gave mine a reassuring squeeze.

"What do we do when Kinneson dies?" Elisabeth asked. "I want to ask your permission for something."

"What's that?"

"I'd like to cremate Kinneson and sprinkle his ashes on Stephen's grave. I think Steve would like that."

"It's a great idea," Sylvia said.

"Sounds good to me. Do we have to put his name on the stone, too?" I meant it as a joke.

"Just do it," Sylvia repeated.

Outside on the busy corner of 17th and Broadway, Sylvia kissed Elisabeth good-bye. Elisabeth and I embraced, neither wanting to stop. I loved her as I loved Stephen. She was my lodestar, my guide to his world. It would be an arduous journey. We hugged and finally let go.

Epilogue

Do You Know Me?

After returning from Florida, my father celebrated his eighty-first birthday—his face thinner, as fragile as dry bone, but still a handsome old man. I brought his grandson, Stephen, with me to the summer house in Narragansett.

"What do you want for your birthday?" Mother asked him.

"Just tomorrow," father replied.

We all smiled. "Always leave them laughing," I said.

"I just want to laugh," he said. "I don't want to leave 'em."

We were sitting on the porch after supper. "I got all A's," eight-year-old Stephen reported to his grandmother. "But next year I'm going to do better. I'm going to get A plus."

"Oh, Stephen, that's wonderful," she said. "You don't have to do any better. Work hard but don't forget to have some fun."

"Can you imagine," my father said. "At my age I still dream of running a 100-yard dash. I'm in the lead but I never seem to reach the tape."

"That's a good sign," I said. "I hope your race never ends."

"You haven't changed, daddy," said mother. "There's a little boy inside of you."

"Oh, no, mother, I've changed," he replied. "I'm more like the horse we used to have. The older she got, the slower she walked. We'd hook her up to my father's junk wagon and the old horse would go "clip-clop" instead of "clippety-clop." She had bladder trouble just like me. And she got lean and haggard... No, the old grey mare ain't what she used to be."

High overhead, three seagulls soared inland, silhouetted against the pale sky. They called to one another, turning in circles, then headed back toward the ocean. What summer memories I had—body surfing in the waves, racing friends on the beach.

I watched father juggle two tennis balls in one hand to entertain Stephen.

"That's good, Poppa," he said. "Can I try?"

Stephen sent the tennis balls bouncing to the floor.

"Don't get discouraged," father said. "It took me a long time to learn to juggle. And I'm eighty-one. You need to practice."

"Poppa, catch." Stephen threw him a ball and my father caught it with an easy motion. He'd been a fine baseball player in his youth.

"Can you do this?" he asked Stephen. He cupped a ball and let it roll down the inside of his arm, then bounced it off his bicep and back to his hand with a quick reflex motion. I loved father's old tricks. Stephen practiced rolling the ball down his arm and by the time we left he managed a couple of catches.

On the long drive home, it began to rain, an old fashioned summer deluge with thunder and lightning and so much water the windshield wipers could barely struggle back and forth. I slowed down and squinted ahead in the premature evening, the dark highway glistening with water. Flash floods had hit

Leominster. An approaching automobile slowly emerged from a puddle like a mysterious marine creature. The storm passed quickly. In the West, a patch of evening sky cleared, pale lavender, before sunset.

"Do you know me, daddy?" Stephen asked.

"Of course," I replied. "Why do you ask?"

"Because I'm adopted. Because I'm not really your son."

"I know you as well as I know anyone in my whole life, sweetheart. You're my son, my only son. You're as real to me as my own mother and father."

"Tell me, daddy." He looked so serious as we drove through wet Leominster streets. "What will I be like when I grow up?"

I tousled his red hair.

"You'll be handsome and you'll be taller than me. And you'll be a good athlete."

"I know," he said, smiling shyly. "I'm good in school, too. What will I do when I grow up?"

"Oh, maybe you'll be a lawyer."

"No, daddy," he replied. "An astronomer-chemist. I want to study about the universe."

I had surely raised my son's eyes heavenward. I leaned over. "Give me a kiss, sweetheart."

"I love you, daddy," he said.

Stephen didn't know how his mother and I were struggling for custody. A son needed his father to help him discover who he was. I was determined to stay in his life.

I parked in the rear lot of my apartment complex. We ran across the courtyard together, racing as we always did to my front door. Stephen splashed right through the puddles. A detour cost me the race.

"I won," Stephen yelled triumphantly.

"Yes, you won," I said. "And your feet are soaking wet. Take off your shoes and socks. Hurry up!"

I switched on the living room light. My apartment needed a good cleaning. There was dust everywhere, floating in the air. It gathered on the floor and furniture, over and under shelves, on the baseboards and appliances. It filled my cave as it had filled all the caves of man. From dust to dust. You had to constantly sweep clean.

"I'll get you some dry socks upstairs."

I rummaged through dresser drawers and found an old pair of my father's wool socks that had shrunk in the last washing. He didn't need them anymore in Florida.

I walked slowly downstairs.

"These are grandpa's socks," I said. "Try them on." Stephen sat on the carpet in the center of the living room. With tears in my eyes, I watched him eagerly pull Poppa's socks over his feet.

The End

Acknowledgments

I owe deep gratitude to Andrea and to Laurel for their love; Joe Winn and Chris Hunter for decades of friendship and support; to Grace Noonan, Corrine Moulds, and the team at Apprentice House Press, thank you for your talent and dedication. To the brave and wise, Kevin Atticks and Jessie Glenn, to Bryn Kristi, Hannah Richards and Kristen Ludwigsen. Thank you all. I am especially grateful to Barbara Olins Alpert for permission to use her portrait of Stephen on the cover.

About the Author

My father died over 40 years ago. I knew he was worried whether I would settle down after my divorce. I had a livelihood to earn and the responsibility of bringing up two children. A child, once, to my father, I have finally grown able enough to serve another generation. He would have loved that.

He was 81 the last year of our life together. That January, I visited him in Florida. Mother said: "Help Daddy with his shower." He was recovering from a stroke. I undressed, got into the shower stall with him. He sat on a stool, holding his four-legged walker, enough room for me to scrub his back. High on his chest, a pacemaker bulged like a hockey puck. I washed his feet, grateful to help him.

My father smelled of Yardley cologne and Desenex powder, iodine and witch hazel. He was fastidious but never vain.

His favorite song: "I'll be seeing you in all the old familiar places"...

He would sing in the car, driving to work or to the beach on a summer weekend. A romantic, an optimist, he had an ear for harmony.

My favorite photo: Dad winning the hundred-yard dash in a track meet, circa 1916, crossing the finish line in a blur of ancient film.

We often drove along a hill overlooking the harbor; below

us, the docks where my father and uncle accumulated cargo for shipment overseas—the dock a toll booth through which scrap iron moved at a few extra dollars per ton. "We need the dock to survive," he explained, "Without export we're just another junk dealer."

Back in 1969, when *Prairie Schooner* published my story, "The 25th Hour," a literary agent wrote to see if I had a book ready; Ginn & Co. used it for a chapter in a High School textbook, *Voices in Literature, Language, and Composition*; and an independent film director in Hollywood asked me to write a screenplay based on the hero. (It got turned down.) *The Readers Digest* paid $3000 for an article about him, which they didn't use. I thought my writing career was about to begin. But it did not. Looking back, I realize that if any of those opportunities had developed I would have never made it through my life at all on what was, basically, a half-full tank of gas.

Coming of age takes a lifetime.

Apprentice
House Press
Loyola University Maryland

Apprentice House Press is the country's only campus-based, student-staffed book publishing company. Directed by professors and industry professionals, it is a nonprofit activity of the Communication Department at Loyola University Maryland.

Using state-of-the-art technology and an experiential learning model of education, Apprentice House publishes books in untraditional ways. This dual responsibility as publishers and educators creates an unprecedented collaborative environment among faculty and students, while teaching tomorrow's editors, designers, and marketers.

Eclectic and provocative, Apprentice House titles intend to entertain as well as spark dialogue on a variety of topics. Financial contributions to sustain the press's work are welcomed. Contributions are tax deductible to the fullest extent allowed by the IRS.

To learn more about Apprentice House books or to obtain submission guidelines, please visit www.apprenticehouse.com.

Apprentice House
Communication Department
Loyola University Maryland
4501 N. Charles Street
Baltimore, MD 21210
410-617-5265
info@apprenticehouse.com
www.apprenticehouse.com

CPSIA information can be obtained
at www.ICGtesting.com
Printed in the USA
JSHW041924240523
42205JS00006B/218